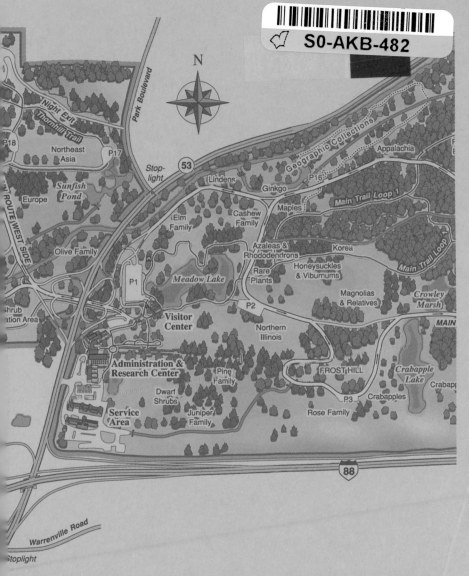

Illustration © 2002 Pulse Design, Inc./Courtesy of The Morton Arboretum

Dear BJ,
I hope these are an
words are an
encouragement
to you!
Love,
Cindy Crosby

By Willoway Brook

EXPLORING THE LANDSCAPE OF PRAYER

Cindy Crosby

PARACLETE PRESS
BREWSTER, MASSACHUSETTS

"The Summer Day" is taken from *House of Light* by Mary Oliver, © 1990 by Mary Oliver. Reprinted by permission of Beacon Press, Boston.

Scripture quotations marked KJV are taken from the *King James Bible*.

Scripture quotations marked The Message are taken from *The Message* by Eugene H. Peterson, © 1993, 1994, 1995, 1996, 2000. Used by permission of NavPress Publishing Group. All rights reserved.

Scripture quotations marked NLT are taken from the *Holy Bible, New Living Translation*, © 1996. Used by permission of Tyndale House Publishers, Inc., Wheaton, Illinois 60189, USA. All rights reserved.

Scripture quotations marked NJB are taken from *The New Jerusalem Bible*, © 1985 and 1999 by Doubleday, a division of Random House, Inc., and Darton, Longman & Todd, Ltd. Used by permission.

Library of Congress Cataloging-in-Publication Data
Crosby, Cindy, 1961–
By Willoway Brook : exploring the landscape of prayer / Cindy Crosby.
  p. c.m.
Includes bibliographical references.
  ISBN 1-55725-320-X
  1. Nature—Religious aspects— Christianity—Meditations. I. Title.
BT695.5.C755 2003
242—dc21   2002154494

10 9 8 7 6 5 4 3 2 1

Published by Paraclete Press
Brewster, Massachusetts
www.paracletepress.com

Printed in the United States of America.

For Jeff

Contents

. . . I don't know exactly what a prayer is.
I do know how to pay attention, how to fall down
into the grass, how to kneel down in the grass,
how to be idle and blessed, how to stroll through the fields,
which is what I have been doing all day.
Tell me, what else should I have done?
Doesn't everything die at last, and too soon?
Tell me, what is it you plan to do
with your one wild and precious life?

—MARY OLIVER
From "The Summer Day"

FOREWORD

It seems, on first consideration, a long shot from prairie to prayer. One fears a leaden book heavy in pieties and thin in real-life detail. But Cindy Crosby does not disappoint. Her meditations on prayer are frank and unsentimental, and her descriptions of the small tract of restored prairie to which she repairs as often as she can are vivid, full of sensory detail, and precise. As she says, "When I die, I want to know I have paid attention." If there is a better way to die, I don't know of it.

Paying attention is the first great connection between prayer and prairies. Prayer is precisely a form of paying attention, which is why Jesus advised that it be practiced not in public but at home in a closet. And prairies are not obviously attractive places. There seems to be an awful lot of grass and sky and not much else. Much of prairie life remains mysteriously hidden. The prairie has been aptly described as a forest in which the canopy lies underground. So to appreciate a prairie, one needs to examine it close-up, preferably on one's knees, in the posture of prayer.

It is also true that to pay attention to anything at all is to invite the unexpected. I once accompanied Hugh Iltis, the great botanist and discoverer of the ancestor of corn, on a trip into a small remnant of Kansas prairie. The other members of the group were mainly fellow botanists, specialists in prairies. What arcane knowledge would Iltis dredge up to impress the group? I wondered. We walked twenty yards into the prairie and Iltis stopped. "I would like you all to find a spot and lie down for fifteen minutes," he said. "I'll tell you when the time is up." We did as we were bidden, feeling a bit foolish. But as we lay there, astonishing things began to happen. From this perspective, the prairie looked suddenly tall. We began to feel the thick cushion of the prairie sod and its moistness in our backs. We began to hear the bobolinks gurgling and the clay sparrows buzzing. There was the constant murmur of wind, reminding us that the dominant plants of the prairie, the grasses, are wind pollinated. The number and diversity of the insects present became apparent. There was the whine of bees, the clatter of grasshoppers. There was the pungently sweet smell of earth. But above all else, a great feeling of peace and contentment with the present fell upon us. For we had been paying attention to the prairie, aided by a new perspective, but we had also been, without knowing it, praying.

This is the epiphany Cindy Crosby reaches as she waits evening after evening for her beloved nighthawks to arrive:

"God, what is this mystery? That I wait, and you fill the waiting with something beautiful, yet unknown to me? That we are here to wait at all, and then we vanish without a trace; frost melting on glass? . . . If I'm not waiting, I miss the best moments. I skim life's surfaces without ever closing my eyes, holding my nose, and taking the full plunge into the depths. I'm willing to take the risk. To be silent and to wait. To listen. To stay open to receive."

Crosby is also describing two parallel kinds of restoration, the restoration of a prayer life gone flat, and the restoration to native vegetation of a tract of land that had been plowed over. Similar labors are involved in each. The seeds have to be planted. The weeds have to be pulled. There has to be a suitable period of waiting. Both involve acts of memory. One has to accept the inevitable burden of imperfection. No restoration is ever the duplicate of its original.

Of these tasks the most interesting is the exercise of memory, since it is the one least practiced in our culture. Crosby has two takes on the subject, in a chapter about the migrations of monarch butterflies, and in one on guide books. It takes, she notes, three or four generations of monarchs to make the annual migration from the United States to a particular fifty acres in the mountains near Mexico City. How is this possible? Despite a good deal of investigation, nobody has the slightest idea. "No answers except this," Crosby says. "They are created with a mysterious blueprint, a memory. A longing for home."

We have worked hard at expunging the idea of longing for home from our culture. One evidence of this the way in which the word "nostalgia" has been turned into a pejorative. To be nostalgic, we believe, is to be cheap, frothy, sentimental. The word has its origins in eighteenth-century Germany, when great numbers of refugees flooded into the country from the east. (My own Polish ancestors were among them.) A striking number of these refugees failed to thrive physically. They were said by the doctors of the day to be suffering from nostalgia, a term coined from the Greek roots and meaning "homesickness."

Is homesickness really a trivial feeling? Crosby thinks not. "Turning my face to the furnace of the west that smokes gossamer clouds of color," she writes, taking her cue from C.S. Lewis, "I watch the dying light tie-dye the sky in lilac, rose, and lemony gold. I want to sail to the ends of the earth where the sky meets the sea; catch a thermal with the monarch butterflies; lift off and cross the continent with the warblers in the fall, moving toward the sunshine, toward spices and peppers, ancient ruins, and starry nights. Gliding toward warmth, and waves, and beaches full of sand. I want to be part of a vast gathering of wings that drifts on wind currents toward the perfect landscape. Toward what I've never known, but remember."

The perfect landscape, of course, is some variation on the one in which we were reared.

Crosby's second take on the work of memory comes as she considers the uses of the guidebooks that she regularly uses, both for nature and for prayer. She begins with an epigraph from C.S. Lewis: "We read to know we are not alone." We read, that is, to validate our own memories. Books of any kind, but especially guidebooks, can help us to affirm or name (which are the same thing) what we have seen, or heard, or felt. The nature guides Crosby has come to rely on began with a bird book, because birds were something she could see from the windows of her suburban home. "Birds," she remarks, "are the first way I eased my homesickness for landscape." As her interests grow, she finds that one, or two, or three guidebooks are not enough. "Of the making—and buying—of books there is no end," she says.

Crosby's guides to prayer tend toward the classics, among them *The Book of Common Prayer*, which, she discovers, requires guides of its own. "The best books on prayer," she says, "are the same as the best field guides—they help me name what I see and what I'm experiencing, and they are companions for the tangled and often lonely paths I walk." And she realizes, in her appreciation of the classic writers, the special power of words repeated across centuries. Words themselves create a powerful kind of collective memory.

But ultimately Crosby finds something incomplete about her guidebooks. They can accompany her on her journeys, in prayer, and in prairie, but they are no substitute for the real thing, for actually praying or encountering in real time and place the actual Baltimore oriole or waving frond of switch grass. The difference, she says, is between learning and knowing. It is only through knowing, she says, "that I make a connection of the heart, something no field guide—no matter how thorough—can tell me how to do."

Crosby's own book, of course, has the same limitation. But the blessing of it is that it will inspire many to make their own connections of the heart, to pray their own prayers, and to find their own places of refuge.

Paul Gruchow

INTRODUCTION

~~~~

Exploring Interior and Exterior Landscapes

I used to believe that to write about landscape you needed to live somewhere surpassingly gorgeous, such as the Rocky Mountains or the Pacific Coast. Imagine my dismay a few years ago to find myself living in the Chicago suburbs, surrounded by shopping malls and interstates. However, like Dorothy in *The Wizard of Oz*, I've found that what I'm looking for is in my own backyard, in a small pocket of the area where I live.

Encouragement came in the words from novelist and poet N. Scott Momaday:

> *Once in his life man ought to concentrate his mind upon the remembered earth. He ought to give himself up to a particular landscape in his experience; to look at it from as many angles as he can, to wonder upon it, to dwell upon it. He ought to imagine that he touches it with his hands at every season and listens to the sounds that are made upon it. He ought to imagine the*

creatures there and all the faintest motions of the wind. He ought to recollect the glare of the moon and the colors of the dawn and the dusk.

Rather than stay unhappy with what I didn't have, I decided to focus on learning the landscape at hand. I write these words to share what I'm learning about prayer, and the tallgrass prairie, and the connection of landscape to our souls. Whatever landscape you are in, whether you are more interested in prayer or in the prairie, I hope that through seeing the possibilities that lie within exterior and interior landscapes, you will discover a greater connection with the God who made them all. Unlocking the secrets of both interior and exterior landscapes is a lifelong venture, and I'm only starting down the path to understanding. There is much to see along the way.

CINDY CROSBY
September 2002

CHAPTER ONE

Mud Season

*I started with surprise and delight. I was in the midst of
a prairie! A world of grass and flowers stretched around me,
rising and falling in gentle undulations, as if an enchanter
had struck the ocean swell, and it was at rest forever.*

—ELIZA STEELE, Summer Journey in the West

*It dawns on me why prayer is the only reasonable practice.…
it is not about our skill or our will,
but rather our humility and helplessness laid bare.*

—WAYNE MULLER, Sabbath

DESPAIR

It's spring, at least by the reckoning of the seasons, but my prayer life hasn't been keeping the same calendar as the one on my kitchen wall. It's stuck in January, and refusing to thaw.

I'm not sure prayer is something you can defrost, but I do wonder if my prayers are consigned to the deep freeze forever. Maybe it's a lack of some interior virtue on my part. Too much busyness?

Something is amiss and I can't put my finger on it.

Without meaningful prayer, my life is full, yet empty. Each day I pack lunches, kiss my husband goodbye as he leaves for work, turn in writing assignments. Let the dog in, let the dog out. The world spins on its axis. The sun rises, the sun sets. Underlying it all is vague, aching desire, a yearning for something more that no earthly activity satisfies.

Though prayer has been the connection to "something more" for me most of my life, giving meaning to routine, lately my prayers have felt cryogenic.

This predicament has caught me by surprise. Prayer has been the steel cable that formed much of my childhood faith structure, as natural as going to church twice on Sunday and often on Wednesday night. My blended Southern Baptist and Methodist heritage hybridized into family prayers that were said regularly at mealtimes, at bedtime, and in times of trouble.

Prayer permeated the lives of my extended family as well. Thanksgiving and Christmas dinners were presided over by my grandfather, whose formal "and bless us now, and our bodies to thy service, Amen," provided a solidly comforting litany that never varied, as predictable as the turkey and dressing that followed.

As evangelicals, we spurned the idea of praying from a book as the Lutherans and Episcopalians did. We didn't need someone else to tell us how to pray, or God forbid, to go through a priest, which is the way we were told the Catholics communed with the Almighty. We wanted direct access, call collect, no operators standing by to help us connect. Give us firsthand conversation with the Lord, who stayed on call day and night.

Although my childhood faith was structured around prayer, I knew many of my school friends prayed differently or not at all. When I accepted invitations to stay for dinner with my best friend Kelly, her mother, a whip-thin dark brunette, would call us to eat. After we settled into our chairs, there would be a momentary pause, for they knew me as a church girl. Kelly's mom would smile and quickly reel off, "Good bread, good meat, good gosh, let's eat!" We'd all giggle and pass the meat loaf. This ritual acknowledged that prayer sometimes preceded a meal without giving a lot of credence to the concept. I usually threw a few silent words of thanks skyward to be sure I had things officially covered, especially if they were serving the morel mushrooms Kelly's dad often brought home from the woods.

I had other friends whose observances were exotic to my evangelical frame of reference. My teenage baby-sitter Sharon, a devout Catholic who corralled me and my unruly siblings when my mother needed rest, often crossed herself—forehead, belly button, shoulder, shoulder—before tucking into the PBJ's and Fritos on the back porch; a ritual I found fascinating, and tried to emulate for myself in the bathroom mirror to get the same effect.

Because I was trained early in faith, prayer came as easily for me as flipping on the television or tying my sneakers. I firmly believed God tuned in to my particular wavelength, waited for me to thank him for the day's bounty, and paid attention as I listed a few needs. The "Now I lay me down to sleep . . ." evolved into "God bless Mommy, Daddy . . ." right down to the gerbils in their cage. I sent up prayers; God, I had no doubt, listened—happy to hear from me, pleased with my compliments, and working with his angels around the clock to assure that my personal needs were taken care of. However, God was not a candy machine—my Sunday School teachers hammered this point home—he knew what was best for me, and acted according to His Will for My Life. Translate: You can pray for the pink Schwinn bicycle, but it might not be in His Perfect Plan, so be ready for the Divine No.

Instinctively, I understood there was more.

One shining week in one particular summer introduced me to a facet of prayer I hadn't seen, an aspect I had never been taught. Eleven years old. I spent a lot of time outdoors, mostly poking around in my backyard, reading in my cave under the forsythia bushes, exploring my grandmother's wooded ravine, and playing baseball with the boys—still too young to care much for romance, I put more thought into hitting doubles and triples. In the midst of this week, without any particular desire or effort, I suddenly heard God's voice coming in loud and clear. The way your FM station sounds when you are driving in the flat prairies of Kansas on a crystalline night, the stars glittering like glass beads scattered on a bolt of black silk. I tuned in. Eleven years old and I *knew*, I knew this was a two-way conversation. I was receiving. God was *there*—O glorious thought, he was really *there*. I was listening, not talking. My awareness was heightened, although the words I heard weren't something I could verbalize. God was with me.

This experience lasted only a brief time. Soon my prayers faded back to rote recitations at mealtimes and bedtimes, or panicky petitions over my best friend ditching me or the big test at school. But the remnants of that glory still cling to me, an unquenchable luminosity that sparks out of the darkest voids.

After a taste of the divine, can you be content with the conventional?

But how do you speak the longings of your heart? When I pray these days, it's like cutting sentences from cardboard with dull scissors. Stiff. Colorless. Despite this, I dutifully continue to pray both out loud and silently. I can't bring myself to eat in a restaurant without blessing the food; it would be like not salting my beef or forgetting to put butter on my baked potato. But in my church community, when we have spontaneous group prayer, I find myself mute. Others wax eloquent, lobbing thanks heavenward, naming crises and begging for intercession. I am empty. For a writer, I am remarkably short on words. When it comes to prayer, I'm reduced to Anne Lamott's "help me, help me, help me," and "thank you, thank you, thank you." And somehow it's not enough.

Thomas Merton, who wrote that "prayer is possible only when prayer is impossible," tells of discovering consolation in two lines from Dom Chapman's *Spiritual Letters*: "Pray as you can and do not try to pray as you can't. Take yourself as you find yourself: start from that."

So I begin where I find myself—by going to my quiet place.

Quiet holy ground for me is the Schulenberg Prairie in the western suburbs of Chicago, a one-hundred-acre tract of land down the road from where I live. It's a place of transition: from native Illinois tallgrass prairie, it was tamed by plow and then tractor to farmland in the past two centuries. Almost all of Illinois' prairie disappeared before recognition of the calamity set in. "We are often not aware of our losses and their value until they are gone," observes the author of *Restoring the Tallgrass Prairie*, and indeed, the alarm rang in Illinois for conservationists far past the eleventh hour.

In 1962, with the vision of Ray Schulenberg, conservationists, and the Morton Arboretum, this spot became only the second area in the United States intentionally planted as native prairie. Reconstructing a prairie is as much art as science. "The land is your canvas; the canvas with your colors—but in the end the painting makes itself, and presents itself in different ways," reflects one prairie restorationist. This land is remaking itself, in constant flux. The ghosts of the past linger in the tallgrass.

It's a place of silence, especially at dusk. It's a place for contemplation.

Sunset. Evensong. The sky dissolves into dark blue bruised with saffron, peach tones on pearl. In the open emerald field, juicy grasses wave knee high, welcoming the dark. Overhead, a red-tailed hawk keens as he spirals upward on a thermal. Late evening light filters through the oak savanna, illuminating the woodsy floor in patterns of jades and limes. The trees are humming with sound: warbles and trills, chucks and whistles. An indigo bunting threads its way from oak to maple, stitching a sapphire streak against a verdant, leafy backdrop. Across the stream, a common yellowthroat and his mate splash color against the dead onyx limb of a walnut tree, chattering their *Witchity! Witchity! Witchity!* Crickets tune up in the grasses.

Fourteen barn swallows, rosy in the sunset, are clipped to the power line with invisible clothespins. Others swoop and dart, fleeting as a sigh, knifing through the air in aerodynamic maneuvers that make my binoculars less than useless.

Winding through this prairie and savanna is Willoway Brook, whose liquid music blends with the song sparrow's clear notes. I sit on the bridge and lean against its wooden planks, which pleasantly scratch my shoulders. The dying sun warms my back. I come here daily to think, to listen, to let creation replenish my soul. Prayer is here in the murmurs of the tallgrass, the blooming of the sunflowers, the chattering of the squirrels in the bur oaks that fringe the prairie. It's impossible not to exalt in the beauty. Impossible to not want to grasp the mystery. Under the hot prairie sun, the prospect of hearing from God again seems conceivable.

"In some real ways, the effort to re-find the landscape, which is the same as the effort to re-attach our lives to the land, is a religious quest," observes Richard Manning in *Grassland*. "The knowledge of the plants lifts a veil. The whole of it is there in the plants to be read, the full soul of a place, its life and the abuses of its life, the creation's intentions and the manifest violations of those intentions."

There's a skin of the landscape I'm beginning to peel back, and I'm finding a map of sorts in the world around me; a landscape of prayer, creation that cannot help but praise the creator. Symbols in the landscape beckon me further up and deeper in. When I'm on the prairie, the barriers come down. My need to stay busy dissolves, my frustrations calm, and I am free to be still.

To wait and listen for the voice I heard as a child.

The tallgrass is opening up different ways of seeing; it's teaching me to pay attention and instructing me in the value of asking questions. Each small step takes me nearer to the prayer life I'm desiring. My apprenticeship is underway.

"The land gets inside us; and we must decide one way or another what this means, what we will do about it," writes Barry Lopez. The landscape is pulling me in and won't let me go. I make up my mind to go along for the ride and see where it takes me.

CHAPTER TWO

Nighthawks

You must not be in the prairie,
but the prairie must be in you.
—WILLIAM A. QUAYLE, The Prairie and the Sea

To pray means to wait for the God who comes. . . .
This coming and his presence are not only the result of our
waiting or a prize for our efforts: they are his decision, based
on his love freely poured out.
—CARLO CARRETTO, The God Who Comes

Waiting

⟊⟋

The first time I saw them, it was broad daylight. Lying on my back on the limestone ledge at the prairie, I contemplated random black dots floating on a sky-blue backdrop, sprinkled like pepper on the puffy cumulus clouds. Some of the black dots were circling in a pattern. Birds, I surmised, flying high. Red-tailed hawks on thermals. It made sense. Yet it continued to gnaw at me: I'd seen redtails enough to know intuitively when something was not a redtail, and the identification didn't slide neatly into my consciousness with a click.

I waited. Then I pulled out my binoculars and continued to study the moving black dots. There were periodic white flashes as they circled in the sun. "Gulls," I hypothesized, but again, gulls being common here, the same vague uneasiness prevailed. I don't have any particular expertise about gulls, but these didn't look like gulls. When you've seen the ordinary enough, you are jarred by the extraordinary.

Soon the dots and flashes disappeared from binocular range. The sky remained blankly blue. I stayed on the limestone ledge for another hour, longing to receive some answers, a little resolution.

Lately I've spent my evenings like pocket change, waiting for something I don't have a name for. They don't always turn up; I live slightly on the edge of expectation. As evening comes, so come the mysterious birds. When the sun disappears below the horizon, I am often left with only my disappointment at an empty sky. But it's worth risking disappointment for chance epiphanies.

I wait for them on the limestone ledge, across from where the bunnies browse, smudged shadows in the tallgrass twilight. The sky melts into sunset. Crickets shake their sleigh bells. Five half-grown mallards murmur to each other as they coast along Willoway Brook, and the life of the prairie shifts from boil to simmer. Goldfinches drop from oak branches to stream bank, and there's a last call for drinks before night's dark comforter is pulled over the creek bed.

Waiting is an open-ended exercise, which I've been cultivating without a lot of direction these days. It's a passive concept on the surface. But the more time I devote to waiting, the more I feel immersed in prayer. Waiting, instead of busying myself telling God what I need and when I need it. Remaining still.

In the evenings, I head toward my waiting spot on the prairie, looking for this stillness. No phones ring, no one asks me to do anything. I walk, and sit, and look, and listen. Finding freedom in the waiting.

Some waiting I do is fraught with anxiety. I'm waiting for my eighty-five-year-old grandfather's body to make up its mind if he will heal or die. He lies in the nursing home with a feeding tube, his body wasted, unable to sit up or even speak much. Waiting. And we wait with him.

In the daytime I manage to ward off thoughts of this by keeping myself busy, but when I wait in that mysterious time slot between the light and the dark, buried emotions often surface. As the prairie grasses catch the final rays of sun and flare for a moment, seed heads brilliant, then fade to black and gray, thoughts in my unconscious are illuminated for a short time. I'm learning I pray best for my grandfather by making this time to wait.

As I wait, I also receive. This doesn't suit me well; I always try to be the first to give, to stay one step ahead. To be the one others are indebted to. If nothing else, I try to keep the exchanges even. If a friend buys me lunch, I make sure I buy the next time. If someone does me a kindness, I try to repay it as quickly as possible. I live in horror of the scales being tipped in the wrong direction.

I'd rather give than receive. It's safer to keep others obligated to me.

Yet to live accepting God's grace is to live in eternal debt. It demands that I wait, I accept, with no chance of keeping the score neatly balanced. It's letting go of control. I'm forced to acknowledge I'll never even things up. I practice solitude, which means staying open to receive. Making time to be alone. Putting things on hold.

A chipmunk skitters along the ledge, then slips beneath the stones. The wind shimmies lightly through the tender foliage under the trees, now blackened by frost, and a chickadee buzzes in the distance. Waiting here has suffused my life with a quiet peace. I'm more centered these days, less frantic, less blown about by stressful events and difficult decisions to be made. Naming my fears, naming my longings, releases them to God in some way I don't understand completely. I only know that waiting here alone, night after night, quenches a nagging, unnamed thirst.

"I find there is a quality to being alone that is incredibly precious," wrote Anne Morrow Lindbergh in *Gift from the Sea*. "Life rushes back into the void, richer, more vivid, fuller than before."

This aloneness gives room for listening. My prayer life has been full of telling God what I want. Petitioning. Reacting to illness, to death, to difficulty. "Protect my kids." "Help me with the difficult assignment." "Give us peace." Now I'm waiting, for what I'm not sure. For life to rush back into the void? I'm looking for something intangible; I trust I'll know it when I find it.

You don't always discover what you look for, I know: I searched the prairie floor in vain this spring for the killdeer's nest; I rummaged through the trees for the oriole's hammock without results. But the joy I feel when I find what I've looked long and hard for is worth days and nights of fruitless searching. And often, moments of great happiness and understanding take me unawares, when I'm not looking. Waiting to see what comes. And perhaps the act of waiting is itself what I've been searching for.

This is new for me, and new insights are always a bit of a shock. But, I want to be shocked a little, caught off guard, jolted from the ordinary. Taken out of the "pending" file and put in the one marked "urgent." I've been marking time. I'm ready for the unexpected. Surprise me. I'm willing to wait.

It came to pass that as I waited, evening after evening, I forgot about the circling black spots in the sky. Once I stopped looking for them, they found me. One evening as I gazed up into the bur oak, listening to a downy woodpecker tap out a drumbeat on the uppermost branch, the first nighthawk crossed the prairie at treetop range. Then another. Six that night. They moved quickly, silently slicing through space, the white bars under their wings a tip-off. Later at home, I paged through my bird book and the puzzle pieces dropped satisfactorily into place. White bars. High flyers. Dark wings. Nighthawks.

One night, it was one nighthawk. And one was enough that particular night. Other evenings I've had to settle for clouds of sparrows or a pair of gawky blue herons, and no nighthawks. Unpredictable. I can't plot them on a flow chart, I can't set my watch by their arrival. They have their own schedules that make no sense to me, and the only way to see them is to make time to wait.

Surprisingly, I've found that my epiphany may be common to others. One evening, some business associates of mine who came for dinner chatted over coffee and apple pie about the landscapes of their youth. One told me how she was reared in the Arizona desert and hated the heat and bleak landscape. When she was transplanted to Michigan she fell in love with its snow and ice. "The best thing about the Midwest is the beautiful cardinals and blue jays," she said. "I was tired of sparrows and nighthawks."

I looked at her, aghast. Tired of nighthawks? What I found so rare, and worth waiting for? I'd had my fill of cardinals and blue jays—they were as ordinary to me as white bread. But my nighthawks—my icons—were as trite to her as a painting of Elvis on black velvet.

We don't consistently see beauty in the same places. What I wait for in expectation is something another may have in full, and what I take for granted, another may long for.

⟿⟞⟞

I wait, expecting. It's right before dusk. There's a tremor of black-winged damselflies in the willows by the creek. The sun drops behind a cloud; shadows vanish. Suddenly the first nighthawk cuts across the sky, then another, then another. A pounding surfeit of nighthawks. Most nights it's been six or eight, silent and moving faster than a blink. Tonight I count ten nighthawks. Twenty. Twenty-five. I count as fast as I can but lose track at thirty-eight. They speed in, a veritable fleet. Their wide mouths scoop insects from the air as they perform bold maneuvers, whirling, wheeling sharply, nose-diving.

I drink my fill, and still they come. Dizzy, dizzy, my vision is blurry and I realize I am holding my breath. I'm tipsy. Adrenaline rush. My cup runneth over with nighthawks. God's unexpected extravagances—why give me one nighthawk tonight when the dusk can overflow with them, spill over the top, and run down the sides? Why does this astonish me?

God, what is this mystery? That I wait, and you fill the waiting with something beautiful, yet previously unknown to me? That we are here to wait at all, and then we vanish without a trace; frost melting on glass? "I am a creature of a day, passing through life as an arrow through the air. I am a spirit come from God and returning to God, just hovering over the great gulf, till, a few moments hence, I am no more seen," John Wesley wrote. "I drop into an unchangeable eternity."

The nighthawks are slipping away. They are here for a brief moment on earth; as a species they are declining, and no one can figure out why. I'm the only one I know who watches for them. If they were gone, would anyone else wait? What vacuum would they leave in their wake, what nameless void that nothing else could fill? Would it be enough if there were only one person waiting for them, one person who would count the sky emptier when they were gone?

One night the writer Annie Dillard lay awake listening to the plaintive call of a bobwhite, bereft of a mate. "Yes, it's tough, it's tough, that goes without saying. But isn't waiting itself and longing a wonder, being played on by wind, sun, and shade?"

Is the act of waiting enough?

If I'm not waiting, I miss the best moments. I skim my life's surface without ever closing my eyes, holding my nose, and taking the full plunge into the depths. I'm willing to take the risk. To be silent and to wait. To listen. To stay open to receive.

More often than not, I think, the nighthawks are around me, cruising at high altitudes out of my range of vision. The angle of light often makes them invisible, much as a spider web slung between branches and glistening with dew disappears when the sun passes behind a cloud. Sometimes I receive extravagantly, other times I'm left with an empty sky. And often I only get flashes of white, glimpses of what I wait for. Coming down to earth—when? I don't know. But much of what I wait for is here, ready to be tapped into if I'm present for it.

Let the nighthawks come.

I'm waiting.

CHAPTER THREE

High Winds

The oldest voice in the world is the wind.

—DONALD CULROSS PEATTIE

If we don't know how or what to pray, it doesn't matter.
(God's Spirit) does our praying in and for us,
making prayer out of our wordless sighs, our aching groans.

—ROMANS 8, The Message

SPIRIT

I've been waiting, I've been listening. Talking to God, however, eludes me. In search of this two-way conversation, I continue to walk on the prairie, where I feel closest to God these days. Hungry, needy for the divine, I keep turning up there, looking for direction and a way to articulate my voiceless prayers.

It's a slate-gray day in March; normally not a day that would beckon me outdoors. But desire for God is an aching void, and I fumble my way late in the afternoon down the path toward the prairie, moving without conscious intention to where we met each other last.

There's a break in the drizzle. Gusts of air almost knock me down. Cold air frosts my lungs; then I breathe it out in a puff of wet, watch it vaporize and be torn away.

High winds rising. Skies like rusted metal. A razor edge of iciness slices through my thin fleece jacket as I walk, then reach the stream bank. I huddle on the wooden bridge over Willoway Brook, pull out my journal, and begin writing, trying to say with my pen what I can't say out loud anymore. Bracing my journal against the whipping wind.

The storm passed over the prairie barely an hour ago, flinging down icy water, drenching the landscape. The wind shrieks and tries to rip the pages from my hand. Two weeks ago, the prairie was burned, a ritual cycle each early spring that fires away the grasses and stimulates the growth of wild-flowers. Already, it's rebounding. Newborn grass stabs through black grit, pieces of which hurl like hail against my face. I'm scoured; I'm scourged. The landscape is blow-dried, scraped, and ransacked, turned inside out, upside down. Anything not anchored securely is snatched up and whisked away.

Locked in a passionate embrace with the wind, the tender grass writhes and moans. The rain has unlocked green from the dead ashes of the prairie; it's fizzing with chlorophyll. Once a sea of sameness, now the emerald fuzz texturizes, takes on angles and ruffles and shapes. Leaves are forming: paddles, crinkles, hearts, ferns. Lances, swords, blades, shields.

There's a sound of trickling water percolating down through the earth, carving creeks as it goes, plowing tears through the terra firma face, seeking the lowest point where Willoway Brook froths and foams, swollen with liquid. In its wake it leaves sudden pools, waterfalls, diminutive puddles. Bubbles spew up from the prairie floor, vomiting cocoa-colored water from unseen underground rivers. The ground throbs, its lifeblood gurgling away.

And too, my prayers are percolating, bubbling. Prayers push against me, pressing. Invisible currents swirl just beneath the surface, looking for release. My pulse thrums heavy with prayer.

Cumulonimbus chases cirrus across the sky overhead. Shadows lie in dark relief on the grasses, then disappear as the sun slides through the clouds. God adjusts the dimmer switch: light, dark, light, dark. Shadows: fading, sharp, fading, sharp, fading, sharp. I'm so close, so far from figuring this out.

I try to form a prayer. "Our Father, who art in heaven. . . ." The wind wails, tearing the words from my lips and shredding them into confetti, scattering them to the four corners of the world.

Goldfinches vibrate through violet-washed air. The smell of saturated earth diffuses through the atmosphere. I'm drenched in scent; then it's torn away from me by the blasts. I'm sandpapered. I'm chapped, burnished by breezes.

On the concrete bridge over the creek, construction sticks are wrapped with neon orange ribbons that flap wildly in the wind. I think of the Tibetans in Nepal who strew the mountains with their prayer flags and prayer wheels, hoping their nonverbal petitions will be heard. Letting their entreaties be carried by the wind.

Next to the bridge, wildflowers are closed against the zephyrs' force. Trout lilies are tight umbrellas snapped shut against the storms. Turning inward, protecting themselves from the wind, they're afraid of being blown inside-out. Wood betony's crinkly leaves are waterlogged, torpid. Plastered with mud and cinders. Vulnerable. Trees bud out in jade filigree, drop pollen, spill bud wrappers in damp mists at their feet. There's a light hail of lime, a shower of burgundy, an emerald precipitation.

A squirrel is momentarily appliquéd against the sky as he leaps against the wind to reach an outstretched branch. He lurches, clutches the limb, grateful.

My prayers are dewy novices. They lurch, they stagger, they grasp, they surge. Words freshly minted yet unsaid, forming in the deep rivers that run through my soul, looking for surface, moving upward, reaching for the current, longing to connect.

A half-grown red-tailed hawk blows out of control over my head. The winds so strong that he can't make any fancy moves, can only hang on for the ride. A juvenile, he's too young, too inexperienced; caught in the power, he doesn't know how to use this force. Fearful of a crash landing. Trying not to come back to earth. His only desire is to catch the wind, but he can't control it. Without the experience he needs, he's unable to ride it, can only be thrown around.

The wind slaps me across the face, unbalances me, presses instability on my gravity. Bend before the force of the wind or break. Lean or be blown away. Brace myself or stagger before this unseen power that moves the world.

"Then after I have poured out my rains again, I will pour out my spirit upon all people," God said to the prophet Joel. I want to be in the current. I want to step out of the shelter. I, too, want to be in the stream, in the force, in the flow. I want to pass through to the beyond.

The Holy Spirit, I sense, is the key.

The wind is water, rushing in currents, pounding like surf. The water is the sky: rippling, moving, singing. Prayers whisper in the hush of fluid, the drumbeat of blood racing through arteries. The grass crests in ocean waves. Prayer oscillates, prayer reverberates, prayer fluctuates, prayer resonates.

The trees begin the chant—all creation cries out. *Would not the very stones cry out?* They do, they do, they say what I cannot. Dry oak leaves are the timpani, freshly sprung larch needles brushing the air with piny resin, maple limbs and hickory branches adding woodwind voices. Listen. *Lord, hear our prayer.* God, hear my prayers.

I'm enveloped in prayer. I open my heart to it. I'm waking up and drowning. I'm falling. Bending. Breaking. Desiring.

Raising my hands to the sky, I lean into the wind, my unspoken words lifting higher, spiraling upward to God. Unspoken, yet connecting.

Unsaid prayer weaves me into the landscape, warping up blades of grass, wisping into clouds, braiding through the bluestem blades, rushing down the creek, polishing the old ivory bones that lie by the stump of the bur oak, sliding with the ribbon snake down the banks to Willoway Brook.

World without end, Amen. Amen.

CHAPTER FOUR

Dragonflies

So much of our life passes in a comfortable blur.
Living on the senses requires an easily triggered sense of marvel,
a little extra energy, and most people are lazy about life.
Life is something that happens to them
while they wait for death.

—DIANE ACKERMAN, A Natural History of the Senses

Prayer is a disciplined dedication to paying attention.

—JOHN H. WESTERHOFF III AND JOHN D. EUSDEN,
The Spiritual Life

ATTENTION

※

$\mathcal{L}$ast night I dreamed of dragonflies, gliding through the haze of my filmy nocturnal imagination with their tensile-strength wings, their titanium lightness of being. When I walk the prairie this morning, thoughts of their fragile-strong bodies catching the currents still drift around the edges of my subconscious. How they slice the air with a delicate crispness. The paths they carve through the tallgrass. I think and think and think of them and almost overlook the reality under my feet.

So much that we miss with our heads in the clouds. So much that we miss in this world.

I see him when I stumble and look down at the mown path to regain my footing. A budded compass plant stalk has been broken and flung at a crazy angle across the trail. The dragonfly is alone. Motionless. Clutching a hairy green wand that bleeds the resinous sap of the *Silphiums*, a sticky gelatinous ooze.

Twelve-spotted skimmer. *Libellula pulchella*. The devil's darning needle. Four wings, dotted with bluish white and bittersweet chocolate, provide a tenuous balance. My shadow falls across his plump chassis, slick coffee-colored armor patched with brown velvet, and I'm sure the shade I cast causes the air around him to cool abruptly. He remains unmoved.

Overhead, his kin float through the grassy fields: half-banded topers glint copper; green clearwings hover like helicopters; damselflies dotted with electric blue neon could light up a marquee. They circle me—a human insect-control tower anchored in a three-foot-wide mown stubble runway through the tallgrass. Touch down briefly on starry campion, then lift. Rise, circle, buzz me, and zip off for places unknown.

Oh, you surges of electricity, crackling through the air! Thunder and lightning. Steel wisps strung on translucent zephyrs.

Crouching, moving tentatively. I know to touch him might be to do harm, yet I can't help myself. My fingers move of their own volition, stretching slowly—oh, please don't fly away—stopping short of one tissued wing, then gently touching the tip. I feel nothing. Transparent, other-worldly. Gossamer ghost. Or only some manifestation of my own wild imaginings? The wing tip bends a fraction, so I know I'm making contact, although my skin can't register sensitivity to something this ethereal.

How do you touch the untouchable? How do you make contact with things not of this world?

Kneeling, knees greening. Marveling at his armored body's intricate structure, plated with loose hinges that give him his gymnastic ability to ply the air, drop down to splatter circles in Willoway Brook, tantalize the kingbird with his crunchy morseled appeal.

When I die, I want to know I have paid attention. To have read creation's journal from cover to cover, and not skimmed the pages. Spent my summer days counting dragonflies, following them across the brook, learning their zig-zag pathways by heart. Made contact with something bigger than myself.

I start to stroke his body, but his ferocious dignity stops me. Respectfully, I brush off my fingertips and scramble to my feet, moving a step back and allowing the sunshine to spill into the void my shadow leaves on the path. I back down the trail until he is swallowed up by the prairie dock's elephant-ear leaves, the rough-laced leaves of compass plants, immersed in tallgrass.

Lucky for you that I'm not a kingbird spotting your corpulent body, a moveable feast, helpless now and grasping at straws in the fields. Lucky for you.

I would surround myself with dragonflies. At home, I dig a shallow pond in my backyard, fill it with water from the hose. Let its muddy bottom cycle through algae—lime, brown, lime, brown. Soon, green duckweed floats on the surface; give duckwood an inch, it will take the beachhead. Arrowhead plants I import take root and multiply with a fecundity that keeps me busy on weekends, pulling them out like dandelions. My lone swamp iris expands in circumference until it's bigger than a bushel basket.

Frogs show up, birds sip and splash, and at last, the dragonflies arrive. Drawn by water; wooed, perhaps, by the little prairie-grass patch I baby along at the corner of the yard. Build it and they will come.

Isn't this what prayer is? Paying attention? Making room for what will come?

These days there's a rock on the banks of Willoway Brook where I while away the hours. Eventually I blend into the scenery, and the dragonflies go about their business, aerial insect crosses moving at a blur, attending to urgent dragon-fly matters as they follow the water's gently curving course.

Two dancers, short-stalked damselflies, are laying eggs together in the center of the creek. They move into an intimate embrace, and he clasps the female behind her neon-blue head with the equally-blue tip of his tail. His body angles up and to the side. His wings rapidly fan the air as he positions her over the shallow mud of the brook, and her jointed back arches in a tight loop as her tail dips down into the mud like an oil derrick: up, down, up, down, planting the seeds of the next generation.

I let an hour slip away as I play the voyeur, watching them repeat the performance. It's another mystery I don't understand, another rite that has gone on for years, perhaps, as I walked the prairie oblivious.

The more I learn, the more opens up. The more I pay attention, the more I find to pay attention to.

A damselfly lands on the stone beside me. We both rest, soaking up sunshine and letting the breeze cool us off. A beetle crawls over the rocks, detouring around us, and a minuscule pale water bug skips across the water's surface in fits and starts.

I don't know their names. I don't know their habits. But the doors to my soul are ajar, and I want to learn, looking up each of their names and repeating them to myself until I have made each one my own. Created a scrapbook of remembered moments to feed my soul, to pull out when winter covers the landscape with ice and snow.

I'm anticipating whatever shows up.

I want to pay attention.

I don't want to miss anything in this world.

CHAPTER FIVE

New Paths

Just when you believe in your own sense of place,
plan on getting lost.

—TERRY TEMPEST WILLIAMS,
Red: Passion and Patience in the Desert

The wildest, most dangerous trails
are always the ones within.

—BELDEN LANE, The Solace of Fierce Landscapes

CHANGE

My quiet place—my prayer place—is under construction.

The entry to the old gravel two-track that starts at Parking Lot 25, meanders through the bur oak savanna, and takes me to Willoway Brook is familiar ground. Walking it is a comforting year-round ritual. This old entry path is where I first found my way to my quiet place with God.

But when I arrive at the parking lot today, it's festooned with yellow hazard ribbons and hot-off-the-press signage. I'm gripped with apprehension.

A sinking feeling of doom.

Slumped behind the steering wheel, I try to take it all in. A large placard featuring drawings of cute chipmunks in hard-hats announces new construction, including a prairie visitors' station, complete with an area to accommodate large tour buses. The entrance to my old path, my favorite path, my familiar path, is barred by a black plastic mesh fence. Signs direct me to a newly mown trail through white oaks and an old field that is in transition between prairie and meadow.

I don't like it.

The familiar is about to change. Many of the touchstones that were important to me are on the old entry trail I can no longer access. The cool larches and pines, the leafy bur oaks. A dead tree where the indigo bunting would wait, its tangle of song tripping all over itself. I had memorized the spot on the old route where batches of snowy white trillium appeared each spring, knew where the goldenrod stems with their swollen galls would rise from the savanna floor. My hiking boots were acquainted with each curve in the gravel walkway, and I could walk to the Schulenberg Prairie with my eyes closed.

Now I'm starting from scratch.

Frustrated.

It's a crossroads of sorts, and I consider my options. The old entry is closed. I can force things—break through the plastic mesh fences, ignore the signs, refuse to adjust to what is happening. Or I can abandon the whole idea of walking out here, go on strike. Quit coming, stop my prairie walks. But my affinity for the land runs deep. I want to be there.

Starting down the new path, I'm hesitant, a bit rebellious. Plagued with questions. A little grieving going on.

Problem is, I'm not partial to change. I like my routines. I make dinner rolls from scratch the way my grandmother did, stubbornly drive my car until the doors fall off, plant heirloom vegetables in my garden. I'm a creature of habit. But now bewildering bird songs float out from the pine fringe along the borders of the mown grass pathway. I'm going to have to get out the bird guide again, tote it with me. Different trees line the edges, mixed with the remembered thick-trunked, luxuriant white oaks and soft-needled larches. New paths, new pieces of the landscape to learn.

A baby cottontail springs out in front of me and scrambles away, mooning me with its white powder puff. I walk until the new walkway ends at the top of the Schulenberg's acreage.

From here, it's a different perspective on the prairie I know so intimately. Early autumn now, and spread out below is a folio of grass, grass, one hundred acres of grass. Grass melds together the landscape, a rippling sea of tans and greens, oscillating with burgundy and flashed with silver. A first flush of asters and goldenrods stipples it with amethyst and mustard. The yellow, sunflower-like blooms of *Silphiums*—compass plant, prairie dock, rosin weed, cup plant—wave above the tallgrass, their stalks thrusting up to a dozen feet into the air.

Spotting an old, familiar path that is still open (thank God, at least this!), I walk down the well-known trail, gravitating toward Willoway Brook. The sound of water, its ability to quench thirst, eternally draws living things with alluring primeval force. Here I spend a quiet hour reclining on a ledge, assimilating the impact of the work that's under way.

The construction is changing the contours of the landscape. Earth-moving equipment arranges and rearranges the bends in Willoway Brook. New rocks are strategically placed midstream. Mown trails offer new angles and vistas from which to view the prairie. The replacement of a weathered wooden bridge with a sturdy iron one is in full swing on the west edge. A proliferation of orange and black plastic webbing laces through the grasses, and the trees sport neon ribbons. Marked for destruction. Ground-down stumps are the only traces left of the once-leafy sentinels that have already met their demise.

A bright red plastic warning sign at the opening of one of my favorite paths warns: "Trail closed. Construction area. *Do not enter.*" I don't like being told where I can't go anymore, especially if the forbidden is a place that used to be home territory. The now-prohibited hill overlooking the prairie where I used to sit and journal is visible through the trees—dotted with pink flags and wooden stakes driven through its heart. More trees wrapped in grim bows. There's a gap where they've bulldozed the spruce copse.

All forbidden ground.

From my vantage point, I see that the progression of the seasons is also creating alterations. Opulent, lush, everything is gorgeous and exuberant. The landscape overflows with flowers. Succulent grasses spray the air with fringed seed heads, bending over the dirt trails, caressing them with their emerald blades. The old, well-worn paths that remain open on the prairie are almost swallowed by fresh greenery, apparently sprouted overnight. Big bluestem leans over the trails, the prairie dropseed curves across, the switchgrass insinuates itself over and around and into them. The known paths are mostly invisible under an avalanche of unchecked growth.

Not invisible to me, however—these old, still-open trails are grooved into my brain. Second nature. Getting to my feet, I walk down a newly mown trail to the edge of the prairie and smack up against a seemingly impenetrable wall of grass. I wade in, sensing the path as I go, letting my hiking boots find the route. All is grass. The feet remember from their habit of being there. They know by instinct and intuition what my eyes can't discern.

I'm feeling my way. Change infuses the air.

The tallgrass touches my bare legs and arms and whispers messages. Prairie dropseed brushes my skin, soft and sensual; then big bluestem whips me with its stiff wands. Switchgrass unfurls its fine seed droplets; silky-looking prairie cordgrass's sharp blades rough my skin. As I wade through mountain mint, I tear off a single leaf, pop it into my mouth, and chew. My mouth floods with menthol: bracing, cool.

I'm wading through this tallgrass prairie, a reconstruction of something once precious and lost. And now it's being overhauled, fiddled with. All in hopes of continued preservation. Old paths eliminated. New paths created. Fresh growth obscuring the well-worn walkways. Some reconfiguration going on, a little redistribution. Change.

As with prayer. It's a beautiful discipline that I've lost somewhere through neglect or not acknowledging its value. I'm re-examining my ideas about prayer. Different paths are opening up, and I'm following them to see where they go.

Gaining fresh insight. Learning new ways of orienting myself in the landscape.

As I walk the detour around a bridge that's being replaced, I hear a thrashing in the reed canary grass. A female red-winged blackbird is tangled in the erosion netting laid on the creek banks. She's terrified, and her frantic, flapping, red-shouldered mate plaintively calls to her nearby. My approach only intensifies their fear, and he screams unintelligibly at me as I bend over the redwing, talking softly.

She instantly goes limp; feigning death or genuinely scared stiff, I don't know. Pulling out my pocketknife, I carefully clip away the green threads wrapped around her leg, anxious not to inflict further injury. Instantly, she is up and away.

They fly off together.

All sorts of questions race through my mind. What if I didn't take that particular path, this hour, on this day? Does my presence here mean so much that a bird is saved from entrapment? If so, what does my absence imply?

The known and the unknown maintain an uneasy truce. Improvements are made, some things are lost. Deaths. Changes. The new paths rarely offer answers to my questions; they only seem to tap into a churning cauldron of more.

These new changes I am dealing with help me discover again my voice in prayer. Frustration greases the vocal cords. I'm learning to articulate my dismay about the remaking of the landscape. As I muse over endless questions, words are unlocked. Wanting God's attention, I'm hammering him with my doubts and uncertainties and grievances.

Change has become a stimulus to prayer.

These new paths—new ways—include making time to wait. Listening, instead of always petitioning God with my requests. Setting aside regular times of the day to pray. Paying attention. The words don't flow easily, but telling God how I *really* feel, the complete, unedited, unvarnished, frustrated version—is giving me a new relationship with the one who made the world around me.

An honest relationship. I'm asking questions. Venting my irritation. Dragging my heels, slowly making changes.

I push through swaths of grass down a path that leads to the lower acreage, walking an old path that is metamorphosing with the construction and the changing seasons.

How fast the landscape alters as the grasses and flowers throw themselves into the arms of early autumn. They offer it all without consideration of what lies ahead—winter's icy caress and the purging flames of the early spring prairie burn. Artlessly, extravagantly, they pour themselves out, thoughtless of the future. Grow. Grow. Grow.

The tallgrass is brimming with prairie dock, huge paddle-shaped leaves sending up thick bare stems ten feet high, creating a green-stalked forest. At the top of each stem are tight swollen fat buds ready to burst into bloom at a moment's notice. Buttery yellow false sunflowers mingle with lavender bergamot and sweep across the landscape, washing it with color. The butterflies are irresistibly drawn to the blooms: yellow tiger swallowtails, buckeyes, cabbage whites, monarchs, sulphurs. It's a chromatic free-for-all, a melee of color. Riot in the grass.

Behind the plastic mesh fences and the red *Do not enter* signs, around the bulldozers that beep from dawn to dusk, on the banks of Willoway Brook trained into new curves and bends, is renewed structure. The surface changes affect it in different ways—the plant mix alters, the wildlife fluctuates—but it's still the prairie. Still built on a solid framework.

If I stick to the habit of being there, keep the appointment, then discomfort, change, is part of the deal. And may give me new perspectives on what I always thought I had known.

The underlying framework is the same, even though routes through it are changing.

The bulldozers train the creek banks into planned curves under a stabilization program, while the red-tailed hawk cruises the drafts over the unburned section of the prairie as its predecessors have done from time immemorial. While the mowers redesign trails, the Baltimore oriole's clear notes in the walnut tree continue to pierce the quiet. A rust-furred iron bridge replaces a tumbledown wooden version, and I cross the one as I once crossed the other, older one. The familiar is dear to me with repetition; the unfamiliar I am coming to grips with. I keep my daily appointment with the landscape as it remakes itself, accepting that it will never be static.

"The miracles of the church seem to me to rest not so much upon faces or voices or healing power coming suddenly near to us from afar off, but upon our perceptions being made finer, so that for a moment our eyes can see and our ears can hear what is there about us always," observed Willa Cather. Through walking untried routes both on the prairie and in prayer, I'm seeing for the first time what has always been around me. Sharpening my senses.

The new paths slowly become routine. I'm exploring. Holding times of quiet and an attitude of paying attention. Cultivating openness to what might appear around the next corner. Finding words to talk to God at last. Adjusting to change.

"Some say change is good, some say not. But since there is no choice about it, I choose to embrace change," writes Robert Hamma in *Earth's Echo*. "If I resist, I will miss the new opportunities it offers and drain myself fighting it."

Each day, as the prairie clock endlessly marks the time, I tick off what's set in motion. The blue heron that flies to its resting spot thirty minutes before the sun drops over the horizon. The white egrets shining brilliantly under the rising moon in the evenings as the days grow shorter. Willoway Brook, limned with swamp sparrows, pocked with dragon-flies. I'm looking for the unknown among the familiar.

I'm moving forward, feeling my way, trying to figure out the next steps. New paths are opening up new ways to pray.

CHAPTER SIX

Monarchs

How utterly astonishing our instant here
(a time scented with dim remembering).
—STEPHEN ROWE, Abiding: Landscape of the Senses

Can you not look around you now and see what is moving
among you? Can you not see what is moving within you?
—ROBERT BENSON, Venite

LONGING

Lately I've been counting monarchs, more by reflex than intention. They coast across my September radar screen, orange and black blips imprinted on blue skies. In my parsley bed the green monarch caterpillars munch; I suspect they're in the milkweed patch in my backyard as well, although they remain camouflaged. As I walk the prairie path early in the evenings, monarchs with stained glass wings sip nectar from the waist-high white boneset blooms.

These Midwestern stops are only short layovers. The monarchs have packed their butterfly bags for Mexico, drawn by an internal homing system pulling them southward.

One of the greatest unsolved mysteries of biology is the migration of the monarch butterfly. How do millions of these butterflies leave each fall from the eastern United States and Canada and end up in a remote fifty acres ten thousand feet up in Mexico's Transverse Neovolcanic Mountains?

"Monarchs are not guided by memory; no single butterfly ever makes the round trip," writes Sue Halpern in *Four Wings and a Prayer*. "Three or four generations separate those that spend one winter in Mexico from those that go there the next. . . . Every fall monarchs pass through my yard, and though I know where they are going, no one can tell me for sure how they get there."

Not only the monarchs are encoded with this yearning— with this remembrance of something they have no memory of. Gray whales migrate seven thousand miles up the Pacific coast from Baja California to the Beaufort Sea; eels descend Eastern streams to spawn and die; before dams, Chinook salmon climb from the Pacific a thousand miles up the Snake River to breed, notes Scott Weidensaul in *Living on the Wind*. How does the warbler wing its way across continents without a road atlas? How does the bar-tailed godwit hitchhike on gale winds six thousand miles from Alaska to New Zealand?

No answers, except this. They are created with a mysterious blueprint, a memory.

A longing for home.

In the face of these mysteries is the recognition that there is more to the world than scientific knowledge and theological conjecture. It's impractical, irrational, inexplicable.

The autumn air is littered with random bits of beauty in flight. Goldenrod is punctuated with the pump of wings, butterflies gorging on a last surge of nectar to refuel for the next leg of their journey.

I sense that I have my fingertips on the pulse of something big. The blind man feeling the elephant. A seasonal synchronization. A larger force is at work keeping it all hanging together, and I can only make guesses about it.

Rational explanations are elusive. Here is something that defies my human scrambling to quantify and define it.

Give me God beyond my imagining. Not a God that I completely understand and can explain, but a God whose depths cannot be fathomed. A God who dreams up the idea of a green caterpillar that would eat leaves, spin a chrysalis and burst from it as an insect with powdered, tissue-thin orange and black wings that soak up sunlight like solar energy panels. A God who gives this butterfly an unerring instinct to warm itself and lift off on a breeze, heading for a home it instinctively longs for, yet knows is there only by faith.

I yearn to know the God who thought this up. The God of unbridled imagination who wants to infiltrate the subterranean caverns of my soul. An enigma— a God ungraspable, impenetrable, and yet personal. A technical virtuoso who sets in motion this massive flurry of butterfly wings, yet an intimate God who knows each swirl in the lines of my fingerprints.

I want to embrace this mystery. To remember the blueprint that's buried within me, the longing for home.

The tallgrass waves over my head in the heat of a fall afternoon as I walk. I wonder, is prayer imprinted in our bones, encrypted in our DNA? Do we tap into some inner vein to release this communication flow with our creator? When God strung our nerves and arteries, did he also string communication cables, optic wires enabling a connection with the divine?

What jump-starts these connections? I don't know, but I'm trying to establish communication as best I can. Praying in brokenness, suffering, loneliness. Praying when I feel joy. I'm moving by instinct as much as anything. Monarchs are caught in a cycle that they never question. . . . I'm caught in an imprinted longing for God I don't understand.

Memory is an iffy thing; with each passing year my short-term memory grows dimmer. But I find my long-term memory for childhood events slowly sharpening. Touch sometimes transports me back; often so does a particular smell. When I use a certain heavy-bowled spoon rescued from my grandmother's silverware drawer after her death, it resurrects memories. Grandma mixed her tea, always Lipton's, with half-and-half, a combination I never cultivated a taste for. She fixed mine straight up with strong applications of sugar. Often we dallied in Grandma's breakfast room, sipping tea in companionable conversation.

This morning when I drank my tea—not Lipton's—and tongued its too-hot liquid from the spoon, the memories of tea sessions enveloped me. The sound of her voice, the strawberry-patterned wallpaper, the smell of the powder she used on her face. The green and red squares of linoleum under my feet as I pattered back and forth from kitchen to table; her terribly wrinkled hand, veined and splotched, pouring the tea; its crepe-paper feel as she brushed against my own smooth hand. She'd scattered seeds on the driveway outside, and we watched the cardinals and blue jays pick through them as we drank our tea. All this I remembered, the memory trapped in the shape of a simple silver spoon, indelibly imprinted in my mind.

"We live in a culture that has lost its memory," writes Gretel Ehrlich. Through prayer, I'm absorbed in reclaiming mine. When I pray, I feel a connection to a memory, the tug of combined prayers of generations before me who have done the same. Waves and waves of prayer that swell behind me, lifting me up, helping me connect through the past to something in my present and my future. "In remembrance is the secret of redemption," a Jewish proverb declares. In remembrance lies mine.

Why does a Stradivarius violin sound so good? "Certain vibrations made over and over for years, along with all the normal aging processes, could make microscopic changes in the wood; we perceive those cellular changes as enriched tone," writes Diane Ackerman in *Natural History of the Senses.* "In poetic terms: The wood remembers."

The sounds of our prayers reverberate; they shape the world we live in. The echoes of the prayers of generations sculpt the spiritual landscape we journey through; we sense something intangible. A memory. It changes us, it remakes our lives, it fires the imagination. It shapes our world, if we let it.

And it's a beautiful world. It tantalizes us with color, sound, touch, and taste. And oh! the smells. The prairie's aroma is *Monarda fistulosa*, wild bergamot or what gardeners call "bee balm." When I suck on its leaves, my mouth tingles with its blend of peppery Earl Grey tea tinged with mint. After the blooms have gone to seed, a dewy morning wi revive the smell, and crushing the seed heads in my han releases its earthy pungency. The fragrance lingers with me long after I leave the prairie.

I also love to mash the lemony yellow coneflower seed heads between my fingers to powder, then breathe in the citrus scent. Aromatherapy for the wilderness-inclined. I come home, and my husband runs his fingers through my hair and inhales deeply. "You smell like the outdoors," he murmurs, the remembered scent of the prairie clinging to my clothes.

The land has a memory, a scent of something that entices us. Walking the Schulenberg Prairie's trails, I see reflections of the past: a shadow of a building's foundation that's left a smudged imprint on the forest floor, a clump of bulbs that once anchored a garden and now has escaped into the wild, the countless corpses absorbed into the ground, death, birth, life, and death cycling endlessly to bring forth more life. Tree stump rings remember the climate of a particular season—wet, dry, wet, wet.

In tandem with a narrative about her mother's battle with cancer, Terry Tempest Williams offers an account of Utah's Great Salt Lake and bird refuges. In the prologue she writes, "Perhaps I am telling this story in an attempt to l myself, to confront what I do not know, to create a path for myself with the idea that 'memory is the only way home.'"

Tapping into this memory, I pray the prayers that have landscaped the souls of millions before me. It's part of my blueprint. It's the way home.

Is it possible to remember the future? I feel this pull toward something to come, as if the fabric of the universe has been ripped, and I can look ahead. My longings make me say yes. The landscape holds a memory and a promise.

It's part of the blueprint, a yearning for the perfect land-scape. Heaven. I desire something I vaguely recall; I long for something in my future that somehow I remember.

Out on the prairie, I lean against the big bur oak shed-ding its collared acorns, and I think about the Chronicles of Narnia books I loved as a child. In *The Voyage of the Dawn Treader,* Prince Caspian and his crew have sailed—almost—to the world's edge, and the big ship will go no further. The children and Reepicheep, drawn by some yearning they can't completely explain, continue on through shallow water until even their little boat is grounded. Reepicheep then drops his tiny coracle into the current and goes on alone. He disappears from the world as he h known it. And sails for the home he has never seen, but believes with all his heart is over the horizon.

Turning my face to the furnace of the west that smokes gossamer clouds of color, I watch the dying light tie-dye the sky in lilac, rose, and lemony gold. I want to sail to the ends of the earth where the sky meets the sea; catch a thermal with the monarch butterflies; lift off and cross the continent with the warblers in the fall, moving toward sunshine, toward spices and peppers, ancient ruins, and starry nights. Gliding toward warmth, and waves, and beaches full of sand. I want to be a part of a vast gathering of wings that drifts on wind currents toward the perfect landscape. Toward what I've never known, but somehow remember.

My prayers mingle with the prayers of those from centuries before, which I remember in some undefinable way. I let my prayers move me into the currents of the memory of what I desire. Pointing me in the direction of what I seek, my prayers slowly propel me toward what I yearn for, joining with the memory of other prayers.

Prayer pulls me toward God, and the memory of something I dimly sense but long to connect with. I lift off with the monarchs, believing in the unknown. On my way home.

CHAPTER SEVEN

Field Guides

*Naming has been for me a powerful way to take into myself
something or someone important to me.
It makes the unknown friendly, approachable, knowable . . .
but where to begin? Nature's enormity, complexity
and variety were overwhelming.*

—MARY BLOCKSMA, Naming Nature

We read to know we are not alone.

—C.S. LEWIS

LEARNING

It began with birds.

My family and I moved to the Chicago suburbs, to a house (one of seven models) in a 1960s subdivision (one of thousands) with a backyard that my newly made friends assured me was huge. After my acreage in Indiana and Tennessee, though, it seemed a doormat.

In Indiana, I washed my dishes and looked out through the kitchen window over three acres of meadow, garden, and woods, bordered by a small creek that ran through the adjoining property. I'd watch the moon come up in the east from the back patio, and coyotes would sometimes startle me in my corn patch.

When we moved to Tennessee, we lived in a house that bordered a wildlife refuge. Our patio overlooked an acre that backed onto a horse farm, and at night, the sky was filled with stars scattered thick as smashed crystal goblet shards.

Ah, but now Chicago. From my kitchen window, I can see four other backyards, and, if the bedroom window is cracked open, the neighbor's patio parties keep us awake long past bedtime. The view includes our ramshackle metal shed. An orange haze smothers the starfields at night.

But there are birds.

Birds are the first way I eased my homesickness for landscape. I hung up as many feeders as I could outside the kitchen window: suet, peanuts, sunflower, thistle, red nectar for the hummingbirds—then spread out a banquet for the birds that preferred to eat their dinner on the ground. I'm now located farther north than I've ever lived, and smack dab in the center of a migratory flyway.

The first autumn, hundreds of birds flew high over our house. I could barely see them, but their cries were loud enough to pierce through the closed kitchen windows. Sandhill cranes, I discovered later through much reading and asking questions, but for a long time, they were an enigma to me. The crows, jays, and cardinals that dropped by the feeders were familiar, but many daily visitors to my backyard were strangers. After discovering the prairie that same autumn, I noted even more puzzling birds I couldn't identify.

I bought *Stokes Field Guide to Birds: Eastern Region* to remedy the situation. Soon I was distinguishing between the different birds that came to the feeders regularly each morning—sparrows, downy woodpeckers, goldfinches, and nuthatches—and putting names to water birds and warblers I saw on my prairie walks.

It was the beginning of a mild obsession. The Stokes was gratifying—for a while. But then we went on a trip out west, and my Eastern Edition didn't cover the magpies and the Stellar's jays I saw there. Plus, I wanted a way to keep track of the birds I was seeing, and there wasn't a check-off list in the back. This was the perfect excuse to buy the *National Geographic Field Guide to the Birds of North America*, which covered all of the United States. It had a bird list in the back, complete with little boxes to check off as I saw each one.

There. I was satisfied.

For the moment.

The large guides seemed to complement each other—the Stokes with its photographs, the National Geographic with its drawings. Still, I was restless with my questions. It wasn't long before Kenn Kaufman's *Birds of North America* came on the market, promising the best of photographs and illustrations combined. More importantly, it was compact, fit easily into my hip pack, and also contained the requisite bird list in the back. My mother-in-law, knowing of my longing, presented it to me for Christmas.

Momentary gratification.

But not enough.

I thought I was adequately covered until we went on a trip to Australia, and its exotic birds flummoxed me. *The Slater Field Guide to Australian Birds* provided a fix and kept me happy for the two weeks we were there. Returning home, I added a few others just to be sure all the bases were covered: a specialty guide for bluebirds, a short-story collection about birds on the East Coast, and a book detailing the best ways to attract birds to your backyard. These were quickly followed by one of the mothers of all field guides, *The Sibley Guide to Bird Life & Behavior*, thicker than our phone book in its oversized format, and stickered with a hefty price tag.

Of the making—and buying—of books there is no end.

Having more than one field guide is alternately perplexing and informative, because each naturalist sees the world through a different perspective and adds something to my own knowledge. Bird calls, for example. Natural Geographic gives the sandhill crane's call as a trumpeting, rattling, "gar-oo-oo," while Stokes calls it a low-pitched "karooo

karooo karoooo." Kaufman doesn't even try, just noting that it's a "guttural crowing rattle." I've tried to emulate the sound for my teenagers—it's a guaranteed way to set them to laughing hysterically—and my version isn't like any of the three descriptions. We all have a piece of it, but in the end, the cranes' sound is indescribable.

Or the kingfisher who sits in the tree by Willoway Brook. All three books tell me it is a solitary bird that can dive to catch a fish in its long bill and that digs tunnels or burrows in stream banks for its nest. But Kaufman mentions another bird I might confuse it with (the blue jay), National Geographic tells me what the juvenile looks like (rust spotting in its breast band), and Stokes details its nesting habits (five to seven eggs), conservation (declining), and extent of its territory (five hundred yards of stream length). Although they differ from each other, all my field guides—on birds, wildflowers, grasses, and insects—add to what I know and help me understand what I'm seeing and experiencing.

My field guides have gaps. Big ones. One of my specialty prairie-plant guides has an entry and photograph for the cup plant, *Silphium perfoliatum,* a distinctive prairie denizen with yellow petal-like ray flowers. It's noteworthy for its opposite leaves, which are joined around the stem to form a cup that holds rainwater. Yet the photograph mostly shows its flowers and fails to show the leaf feature for which it is named. It's up to me to do a little detective work and fill in the blanks.

Although my field guides are imperfect, using them as a reference to help me name what I see *is* a powerful way to start. Any good field guide will help me identify what it is I am confused about, and then tell me some history, place it in context, describe its habits, and—if it's a really good guide— offer anecdotes from the author's experience.

～～✕～～

As I learn to pray, books are often my wisest teachers, my mentors, my friends. Certain books have become my field guides to facilitating my understanding of prayer and landscape as spiritual connections to God. When I read that other pilgrims throughout the centuries are mystified by prayer, or went through periods when prayer took a vacation, I relax and despair a little less. I know there are names for what I am experiencing.

When I first began exploring the idea of praying regularly at certain times of the day, or *fixed-hour prayer* as it is sometimes called, I was intent on developing a "habit of place" for meeting God in my interior landscape. The classic way to do this was to begin with a seemingly simple red volume, *The Book of Common Prayer*, or the BCP. When I opened it for the first time, I realized I was in trouble. It was bewildering. Intimidating. Someone called an *officiant* appears frequently, a sort of leader, but I was doing this on my own time. Not a leader in sight. The back section was full of prayers for things such as "Burial of the Dead," not applicable unless I was laying to rest one of my children's numerous pets.

And all the references to "Martyrs" and "Rites" and "sets of Suffrages"—what was all this about? Then a "Collect of the Day." Catchy phrase, but what did it mean? Did I pick and choose? And what was a "Collect?"

To figure out the right "cycle," whatever this was, I had to decide if I was in Year A, B, or C, which I was instructed to do by determining if the current year was divisible by three. Math is not my strong point, and this little additional requirement did not endear me to the BCP. When I got to the tables in the back for finding "Holy Days" (good Lord, what is a "Holy Day"?) I was genuinely frustrated. I wanted to establish a habit of prayer, and these types of complications made me almost throw in the towel before I'd begun.

Robert Benson's *Venite* first demystified fixed-hour prayer for me with his simple guidelines, his gentle words, and his interpretation of the "offices" (not a building, by the way, but a set of prayers). Benson writes in his preface, "Finding your way to the daily practice of the ancient daily prayer through these books is so difficult that almost anyone who attempts it on their own is usually discouraged and likely to finally give it up." I felt understood.

With practice, flipping back and forth to the right spots in *Venite,* using a few bookmarks to keep my place at each section, I began attempting the habit of "fixed-hour prayer." And immediately I felt the peace that comes with finding something I longed for but never could articulate. A pull toward something greater than myself.

Yet, for someone unfamiliar with liturgy, there was still a lot of page-flipping going on in *Venite.* When I discovered Phyllis Tickle's *Divine Hours* series in three volumes, I found it further simplified things. The day's prayers are laid out in order for each day, with the bedtime prayers—compline—

grouped together by month. I only need one ribbon to mark my place. It complemented *Venite,* with its daily reminders to pray by name for those I loved paired with Benson's beautiful interpretations of the readings. And *Venite* and *The Divine Hours* didn't assume, as the BCP did, that there was a leader involved—everything was set forth for the solitary beginner committed to learning to pray. Me.

With the idea that I was going to pray at certain times of the day, portability was fast becoming an issue. I loved *The Divine Hours,* but in order to spell everything out and minimize the page turning, the three books in the series (*Autumn/Winter, Spring, Summer*) were fairly large. Toting a volume out on my walks or when backpacking was out of the question. *Venite* and the BCP both have the advantage of being, respectively, thin and compact, so when I travel or am walking, I usually slide one or the other into my hip pack. If I'm backpacking, where every ounce counts, I photocopy the pages of the appropriate section of *The Divine Hours.*

As with my bird field guides, my prayer guides soon expanded to include books that advised me in the particularities of my new discipline. *Sabbath* by Wayne Muller teaches me how to let go of my busyness and come to the idea of rest with intentionality. It helps me slow down and get rid of some of the hyper, nonstop activity coming between me and time to pray. Two small books, *A Guide to Prayer for All God's People* and *A Guide to Prayer for Ministers and Other Servants*, affectionately referred to as "The Red Book" and "The Blue Book," have excerpts from both ancient and contemporary writings on prayer, organized by topic. Not only do they introduce me to many new authors, they are small and fit into my hip pack. Lorraine Kisly's *Watch and Pray* furthers my acquaintance with writers on prayer, and because it's larger than my red and blue books, it's a good nightstand reference rather than a carry-along.

In *The Interior Castle*, St. Teresa of Avila counts the reading of good books as one of the key ways that God's appeals come through to us. I read and know I'm not alone; I'm part of an extensive community that through the ages has longed to communicate with the creator and stumbles blindly about in the quest to do so. Good books put a name to what I can't articulate. And by naming my need for prayer, and discovering ways to reach across the void to God, I become better acquainted with my soul. I develop an appreciation for prayer in all its different facets. The best books on prayer are the same as the best field guides—they help me name what I see and what I'm experiencing, and they are companions for the tangled and often lonely pathways I walk.

For most of my spiritual guidance about prayer, I tend to look to the older field guides—the classics—which have gained a patina possible only through hundreds of years of assisting spiritual seekers with their prayers. The Desert Fathers and Mothers, Thomas à Kempis, Teresa of Avila— these are writers I missed growing up but found in midlife. They taught me that that nothing I wrestle with in learning to pray is new, that prayer is a long learning process developed in small, baby steps, and most important, that the practice of prayer is a lifetime commitment.

As a wordsmith by vocation, it astounds me that it has taken me this long to understand the power of words repeated throughout the centuries by those also longing to draw nearer to God. But still, I tend to overspiritualize the ancient writers, to believe that it was somehow easier to pray "way back when."

Contemporary writers of prayer guides have the advantage of knowing the particular challenges of the world I live and breathe in, and they write about a life of prayer in light of things Teresa of Avila or Thomas à Kempis could never have dreamed of. Katherine Norris's *The Cloister Walk,* Phyllis Tickle's *The Shaping of a Life,* and Benson's *Living Prayer,* with their personal descriptions of learning the discipline of prayer, are intimate companions for the journey. Reading a first-person contemporary account of someone who comes to grips with the need to pray gives me encouragement that even in this busy life, it can be done.

Writing down my own observations also helps. Because I can't lug all my field guides out to the prairie with me, I take a journal. It is there that I scribble indecipherable sentences describing what I see and draw anatomically incorrect pictures of dragonflies, butterflies, and unusual flowers. Back at home, I skim through my field guides. In addition, I describe to my mentors what I'm stymied by and ask for their opinions. I let others inform me, yet I take their words and pair them with my own observations and experiences to come to my conclusions.

Writing is a way I figure out where I'm struggling. When I journal through a difficult circumstance, or write through a troubled time in my life or about something that I know needs to change, the act of naming it and writing it brings me closer to resolution.

Yet no field guides or writing about my observations replace the act of prayer. For a while, I was content to write in my journal and read about prayer rather than to actually pray. Empathy for this situation came, unsurprisingly, through yet another book. I found consolation reading Thomas Merton's sheepish words in his journal, *The Sign of Jonas,* "As usual I have to check my appetite for books and work and keep close to God in prayer."

If I sat in my living room and read about the Baltimore orioles on the prairie, I would have the factual information. But it's not until I make the practical connection--that I stand in mud under a tree looking through the leaves for the oriole, hear its song day after day from the limestone ledge, spend hours tramping through the prairie's fringes and margins looking for its distinctive hanging nest, figure out its habits (what it likes to eat, what trees it prefers) and sketch it into my journal—that I make the transition from *learning* about the Baltimore oriole to *knowing* the Baltimore oriole.

It's then that I make a connection of the heart, something that no field guide—no matter how thorough—can tell me how to do. Making these connections on the prairie and in prayer come only through personal experience. I'm only beginning to fill in these gaps for myself. And I'm beginning to realize I can't do it alone.

CHAPTER EIGHT

Pulling Weeds

That land is a community is the basic concept of ecology.
—ALDO LEOPOLD, Sand County Almanac

Christian prayer is above all the prayer of the whole human community, which Christ joins to himself.
—THE LITURGY OF THE HOURS

COMMUNITY

❧

I know that the prayers of those who have gone before me are part of the structure that is informing my new life of prayer. Yet I have experienced little community in a way that stimulates me to understand prayer. Not knowing quite how to begin, I search for community on the prairie.

The arboretum is closed. The hot, humid day is handing its keys to cool evening, and out on the Schulenberg Prairie a group of volunteers are planting swamp saxifrage and prairie plantain. My hands are muddy, and the moist area I'm working in is full of water draining off the upper fields from the long, gray month of rains that quit only yesterday. Overhead, goldfinches are chattering in high-pitched voices to each other about the events of the day, and across the gravel road, a few volunteers laugh as they plug rare plants into the ground. A red-tailed hawk swirls through the air currents overhead, looking for anything edible our efforts might have flushed through the foliage.

It's May, and the first meeting of the year for the arboretum's prairie volunteers. Almost twenty-five people have turned out to help weed, plant, and keep the prairie in good shape. Long after the arboretum's iron gates have clanged shut, we'll keep on working until sunset. The previous summer I often saw the group getting ready to work, and I vowed I'd show up next year and see what it was all about. This summer I came, I saw, I planted; I'm hooked.

"Do you want the shovel?" calls Julie from across the road. I assure her my trowel is working fine, and keep digging. The prairie plantain has a slightly bigger root system than the swamp saxifrage, and the bank in the water run-off area is blanketed with erosion mat and stones. Bracing my boots against the bank, I keep chiseling away at the hole.

For one who loves to come to the prairie to reflect, to rest, and to find silence, these summer evenings are a cause for readjustment. I've thought of the prairie as a place for solitude. Now I'm seeing it as a place for community. Together, we're doing in two hours what it would take an individual weeks to accomplish. Although some of these folks have been coming out for years to volunteer on the prairie, for about half of us this is out of the ordinary. Through working side by side in the mud, we're already forging a common bond. United by tallgrass.

The power of community is new for me, both on the prairie and in prayer. For a long time, I was unwilling to volunteer and associate my quiet place with a place of work and people. After I've spent a summer investing some sweat into it, I've found that working with a community of those who also care about this particular prairie has intensified my relationship to the landscape rather than spoiling its niche for me as contemplative ground.

This is no small breakthrough. I used to be put off by community, especially in prayer. I don't like to pray out loud in a public setting, and I'm usually silent in group prayer as others spontaneously speak their petitions and their praises. Putting thoughts together orally eludes me. More likely than not, I am mentally rehearsing what to say.

When I do pray spontaneously with certain people— who pray as the spirit moves—I find myself, eyes closed, inadvertently speaking at the same time as someone else. An awkward silence follows, then a hissed, "Go ahead." "Oh, no, please, you go." "No, it's okay, go ahead." Not exactly an encounter with the divine.

Recently my family joined a church community whose regular morning service includes reciting the Lord's Prayer together. As I chant the well-worn words "Our Father, Who art in heaven, hallowed be thy name . . ." something unlocks inside me. When I close my eyes and repeat the words of centuries, I experience a connection with community that has eluded me for many years.

It's not only me. A friend of mine tells me she is feeling estranged from God these days, and unable to pray on her own. When she tries to run through the liturgical prayers she's learned by heart, the words scramble up in her brain. Yet when she sits with her church family on Sunday morning and the prayers are recited together, the words effortlessly trip off her lips. The dynamic of the whole, the synergy of the group prayer, is what allows her to connect with the words that confound her in private. It's a regular affirmation each week of a need for each other.

As prairie volunteers, we meet at the appointed time, we sweat, we bleed, and we get muddy together. Weeds are pulled, paths are cleared, and plants are tucked into the dirt, snug in their permanent locations. Sometimes it feels like progress; other days we look at each other at the end of the evening and wonder if we've accomplished a thing. But our actions build on the work accomplished by countless laborers before us, all with a vision of what could be done, a faith that this landscape could be reconstructed to resemble its original splendor. Working together.

Praying the Lord's Prayer, the psalms, and other traditional prayers alone at set hours during the day allows me to feel the invisible community of others all over the world, praying around the clock words that are two thousand years old. I feel the pull of this community, a supernatural strength of numbers, an energy force greater than my words and myself. I can lean on the prayers that have gone before me, the prayers said alongside me, the prayers that will continue long after my lips have ceased to utter another sentence. I'm a link in an unbroken chain that is greater than myself; building on the work of centuries and unfinished in my lifetime.

Each Tuesday evening before darkness closes in, the veteran prairie volunteers in the group take us on a little educational walking tour. Tonight it's a swing through the late-May blooming plants—pink shooting stars, spiky cream wild indigo, sky blue Jacob's ladder, and gangs of violets in purple and white. A breeze ruffles the knee-high plants, while in the west the sky flies its silken sunset banners, reflecting the colors of the flowers below.

I thought I knew the prairie plants well, but already I learn I've misidentified one plant as golden Alexander, *Zizia aurea,* and it's prairie parsley, *Polytaenia nuttallii*. "Look at the leaves," urges Marj, whose acquaintance with the prairie spans several decades. "See the difference?" Now that she points it out, I guess I can. I tuck this information away and then ask her about a one-inch high mat of white flowers with alternate leaves that has eluded my identification, despite all my field guides. "Oh that," she says, waving her hands like it's a no-brainer. "Bastard toadflax."

Well. That's one mystery cleared up.

As the summer progresses, we move from planting diverse prairie specimens to ridding the prairie of the plants that will eventually crowd out the desirable ones. July evenings are spent pulling sweet clover, *Melilotus alba,* a long-term offender. At one time it was a positive, intentional presence in the landscape. When the Schulenberg Prairie was a farm, sweet clover was a good nitrogen fixer for the soil and was planted as a rotation crop.

When the prairie restoration began in the early sixties, the sweet clover swiftly transformed into a raging liability. Left to its own devices, it quickly blankets an area, choking out native plants and insolently waving its white lacy wands. It's particularly interested in exploiting the edges of the mown paths and any "wounds" that appear on the prairie, gouged out by natural elements or human interference.

Bent over in the waist-high bluestem and switchgrass at the end of July, I concentrate on one small area around me, ridding it of sweet clover. The smaller shoots and knee-high plants come out easily. Larger plants, especially those up to my shoulder, are more stubborn. Their taproots grasp the dry prairie soil with a tenacity that defies my steady pull. I dig in my heels, grip the base of the plant, and lean back, all my weight aligned against this menace. My hands slide along the thick stems, and I feel something begin to give. Then, *snap!* I almost fall backward as the clover comes off in my hands. But not the root.

Removing only the part of the plant that grows on the surface is an aesthetic, but temporary, solution. Where one stem was, three will spring up. The tap-root has a survivalist mentality. Now I have to dig out the taproot or clip the stem at least at the soil line to forestall its return. I opt for cutting it off. A little dirt scraped away, a couple of snips, and it's finished.

I pick up the clover plant and toss it in the pile, then arch my aching back and mop my forehead with my bandanna. The sun is setting, and the white flowers on the prairie are lit up with a last-light brilliance. Including the clover. As I look across the prairie toward the savanna, it appears in waves and waves . . . *ad infinitum*. It's enough to make me despair.

But I don't, because I'm not in this alone. Working with me, forming a broken line, are twenty-plus other volunteers, all wrestling with their own patches of sweet clover, all bent on obliterating the enemy. By myself, I could pull clover all summer, twenty-four hours a day, and likely not make a dent in it. Our combined labor brings about substantial progress.

The prairie itself is an interconnected network of grasses and flowers, soil and water, fire and weather, birds and mammals, insects and people. It is at its best when everything is working together. When one piece of the whole is out of kilter, it triggers a domino effect. Let the wild lupine, *Lupinus perennis*, disappear from some prairie remnants, and the Karner blue butterfly, whose larvae prefer this particula plant, loses one of its primary sources of life. Sweet clover creeps in on the Schulenberg Prairie, and soon the richness of native plant life has vanished. The annual burn changes the vole and mouse populations. Willoway Brook runs low, and the dragonflies and damselflies swarm to lay their eggs in the shallows. It's a community of change. Each action influences another; each member of the community builds upon the efforts of the whole.

Charm in the singular, beauty in the aggregate. Significance in the single cardinal song that pours out into the landscape, and glory in the flock of cedar waxwings' soft music as they congregate in the evenings by Willoway Brook. Without the individual, the opportunity for landscape is lost. Without the landscape, context for the individual vanishes.

A dependency that I once resisted forms in my life. Now it becomes strangely alluring. Community prayer is powerful. The prayers of many form a woven net to catch us, to hold us, and to encourage us when we falter.

"We know well enough that every finger of the hand has a use that is separate and that no finger could do so well," William Bryant Logan writes in *Dirt*. "Yet even to do that, the community, the ensemble, is primary. And through the neighborly relation of parts, the hands perform those functions of which prayer is the plainest manifestation: to dig down, to grasp, to lift, and to let go."

Through the efforts of many: planting, replanting, and pulling weeds, the prairie will continue to sustain community.

The single red-tailed hawk I see regularly on my prairie walks showed up with two others in tow this week. Although each hawk spiraled on different levels of a thermal, they soared together over the prairie, shrieking to one another, flying over the tallgrass mingled with white sweet clover that defied our group efforts. Sharing the thermals that whorl them ever higher, they have learned how to live in community. I'm learning to do the same.

CHAPTER NINE

Compass Plants

Grass is the forgiveness of nature—her constant benediction.

—JOHN JAMES INGALLS, "In Praise of Blue Grass"

*Repentance is not a popular word these days, but
I believe that any of us recognize it when it strikes us in
the gut. Repentance is coming to our senses, seeing, suddenly,
what we've done that we might not have done,
or recognizing… that the problem is not in what we do
but in what we become.*

—KATHLEEN NORRIS, The Cloister Walk

CONFESSION

I've regretted many things in my life, but never watching a sunset. Tonight I make time for the early evening pageantry. At home the family is fed, the dishes are washed, and the kids are busy checking e-mail and talking on the phone. Community and family are things I cherish, but after a day full of both, I'm looking forward to slipping away to the prairie for a little solitude.

As I walk through the tallgrass this evening, the sky splits open like a milkweed pod, slipping its silks into the dying light to be combed by the wind into long, cirrus strands. Tonight it backlights the acres and acres of blooming compass plants, leaves all aligned in the same direction.

Pick up any book about the prairie, and sooner or later you'll read about the compass plant, *Silphium laciniatum*. It's a prairie icon. The basal leaves are coarsely cut—deeply divided, flat, and perhaps second only to prairie dock in size. They resemble large, elongated oak leaves. The compass plant's thick, bristly stem skyrockets up to a dozen feet tall in overtopping the grasses and forbs, reaching for sunshine.

It's topped with alternating flowerheads similar to small yellow sunflowers.

The hairy stems bleed sap, which Native Americans used as gum. I like to gather the sparkling rosin beads from the wounded stems and chew the resulting piny-tasting wad. After a little mastication, it resembles Wrigley's spearmint. If the rosin beads are newly leaked, they melt on my fingers, making them tacky as super glue. I stick to everything I come in contact with until I'm back home and able to scrub the sap off of my hands.

I tried to grow compass plants in my garden at home without much success—the rabbits thought I was growing a salad bar for their enjoyment—and so I consoled myself for a long time with the proliferation of compass plants out on the Schulenberg Prairie. If I couldn't have them in my backyard, then at least here.

This July, as in all Julys, the compass plants reach shoulder height and begin to bloom. But as soon as the flower-fest begins, the budding flowers start dying *en masse.*

Horrified, I examine a compass plant. Its flower stem are partially severed; the wounds leak resinous sap. T flower buds sag and are already turning to brown. All are me the same scenario is enacted. Compass plants are dying, and I don't know why.

It takes a village to answer all my questions. As was his habit, prairie manager Craig Johnson took our volunteer group on a walk at sunset one evening, after we were pleasantly exhausted from weeding the sweet white clover and ragweed. Pausing by a compass plant, half its flowers drooping, severed, and dying, he explained that the *Silphiums*, particularly the compass plant, host parasites. Among these are mordellid larvae, which tunnel through the flowering stems. As adult weevils, they clip off the compass plant blooms and lay eggs in the flowers. The dying flower head becomes their weevil nursery.

All is not lost, however. Even as the weevils wreak havoc, the plant is quietly putting out another set of unspoiled buds. These wait, tight and curled, until the weevil has done its work below. Then they burst into bloom.

Compass plants have a fierce determination to overcome numerous setbacks. It makes me think of the poet May Sarton, who in her battles with depression found comfort in these lines: "I think the secret of much of the unrest and dissatisfaction with one's self and longing for a more vivid, expressive existence is the thing planted deep in everyone—turning toward the sun, the love of a virtue and splendor that must be adored. . . . One is always trying to tune one's self to an unheard perfection."

The compass plants work with what they've got, striving for perfection despite their flaws. Overcoming apparent disaster, they burst forth in as many as a hundred blooms. Their bright yellow rays illuminate the prairie like thousands of small triumphant suns, more glorious for the attacks they have weathered. When the seeds finally ripen in early October, I spend autumn afternoons watching goldfinches perched on compass plant stalks, enjoying their snacks.

Tonight I stop and rest on the limestone ledge overlooking Willoway Brook. The air is fresh and clean smelling; the sheets of the day are hung out to dry on the line of night until morning, when they'll be shaken out to cover the landscape again. The sun's gold coin drops into the slot of the horizon as the blue sky dissolves to apricot and lavender.

These peaceful evenings on the prairie are a time of quiet self-examination. Looking at the little destructive things in my own life. Taking my faults out one by one, I relentlessly sort through them. Jealousy. Wanting what a friend has. Impatience. Anger. Failure to forgive a family member who wronged me. Serious selfishness issues. Other sins that I name silently but don't dare write in my journal. The limestone ledge becomes my confessional as I wait for God to bring each troublesome fault to light. I wrestle with the darkness in the landscape of my soul.

My shortcomings separate me from the one I want to know. Little sins that don't seem like much at the time build up until they form a logjam that freezes my communication with my creator. Recognizing my deficiencies is more diffi-cult than it sounds—I'm an expert in cover-up, proficient in the art of delusion, rationalization.

Until things start to wither. Go wrong. Collapse. Often I'm at the point of positive change, only to abruptly lapse back into my old habits, like the compass plant flowers withering as they are trying to bloom. I feel disillusioned and disappointed and horrified by turns. It's then that a regular time of self-examination and confession induces honesty; it calls up my true shortcomings from the darkness to the light. I look at the marks on my soul, and it's the same sins I keep seeing, over and over. Ingrained habits shoved down to unfathomable levels, grooved into my psyche. Rearing their ugly heads in the light of day.

The seven deadly sins according to Christian tradition are pride, anger, envy, gluttony, lust, sloth, and covetousness. I have more than a nodding acquaintance with them all; and some seem to have taken up permanent residency. I acknowledge the places where I've wronged another, said a sharp word, envied a friend—all little sins, I tell myself, barely visible ones. The more time that passes while I tolerate a particular shortcoming, the more it is subtly interlaced into my life, tangling me into a net of my own construction. Just as with poison, "a regimen of small doses is usually what kills us," writes Garret Keizer in *The Enigma of Anger*. A regimen of small doses of sin has kept me from praying in the way that I long to. Their cumulative power is formidable. Burrowing into my soul, they abruptly cut off my chance to be the person I desire. To be the person I want to become, I have to deal with these sins, do some damage control.

Bringing them out into the light and grieving over my faults compels me to throw myself straight into the arms of the one who loves me most; the only one who can make me clean again. It's the first step in the elimination process: a recognition of my imperfections and a longing for grace.

"Be prepared. You're up against far more than you can handle on your own," the apostle Paul wrote. "Take all the help you can get, every weapon God has issued, so that when it's all over but the shouting, you'll still be on your feet. . . . Prayer is essential in this ongoing warfare. Pray hard and long . . . . Keep your eyes open."

Even when my eyes are open, I am tempted to wall off the pain caused by my imperfections. It's a protective mechanism. I have to unlearn this. Pull the barriers down, and let myself experience the emotions my wrongs have elicited. When at last I feel the grief of my failures, I'm ready to ask for forgiveness.

My eyes are open. The walls are coming down.

The power of landscape excavates these emotions. Tears come easily, the thin veneer of being "on" for whoever is around is peeled away. The prairie is a safe place for me to cry. I am willing to exhale, to not "buck up and keep strong." To admit the anguish of what I've done.

What would a sinless life look like? I can only imagine. Strive as I may, I won't achieve it. My interior landscape is scarred. I identify with Sisyphus, rolling the boulder up the mountain only to watch it break from my grasp and go rolling down again. Not even three steps forward, two steps back. More like devastating falls and crashing disappointments in myself.

Occasionally I rush through confession. But to be *truly* sorry, to grieve faults, I must stop myself, find a place of quiet, and take time—time to imagine what the effect of the thing I've said, or done, or thought, has been on myself or another. Time to grasp what making even a small bad choice means. Suffering genuine sorrow. Changing my attitude. Not confessing as a selfish desire to wipe the slate clean to make myself feel better.

The most compelling aspect of the compass plant is the position of its leaves, which loosely point north and south. To see the prairie at sunset with the coarse compass plant leaves backlit by the dying light, all pointing the same direction, is to join yourself with the Native Americans who likely paused at the same portent of something greater than themselves.

I try to keep pointed in the right direction. Keep my focus on where I'm headed. Taking my cues from the compass plant, and from my time spent in self-examination.

Reformed alcoholic and former Catholic priest Brennan Manning writes:

> *Confession becomes more than a "Minit-Wash," more than a sigh of relief for summoning the courage and the humility necessary for honest self-disclosure, more than mere satisfaction. . . . It becomes a joyful return to the Father's house, a reconciliation with the Christian community in a spirit of atonement and gratitude, a building of the love-relationship with God and our fellow human beings which sin had attacked, a reopening of the human heart, and a renewed possibility for the full, definitive flowering of the Christian personality in the wisdom of tenderness.*

Confession followed by grieving my faults offers me this potential for a "full, definitive flowering." As Kathleen Norris, *The Cloister Walk*, reminds me, "Repentance is valuable because it opens in us the idea of change." I've resisted change in my life, but I'm acknowledging my need for it now.

When I miss my time of confession through prayer, I'm scattered like the clouds, blown by the wind. Cast adrift. My faults, my sins, are what separate me from a God who is holy. Prayer is, as Eugene Peterson writes, "the action that integrates the inside and the outside of life." It keeps me from straying too far off course. At day's end, I pray the Daily Office's Compline, which brings me a sense of completion. It starts with confession:

> *Almighty God, my heavenly Father: I have sinned against you, through my own fault, in thought, and word, and deed, and in what I have left undone. For the sake of your Son our Lord Jesus Christ, forgive me all my offenses; and grant that I may serve you in newness of life, to the glory of your Name. Amen.*

Confessing, spilling tears. Finding renewed faith in God's aggressive grace in the light of my shortcoming "There is a distinct comfort in being known, is there no asks Keizer. It's this recognition that I am known by G deeply known, down to all of my grubby little imperfections; that I'm welcomed and accepted by him anyway, that satisfies deep longings and comforts me in a way nothing else can do. Because of grace. "Grace . . . invites us into life--a life that goes on and on and on, world without end," as Paul says in the biblical book of Romans.

Grace. Forgiveness. The bitter disappointments of my shortcomings are mitigated by both.

I immerse myself in the world's fleeting moments of beauty, glimpses of the eternal. My inner well is full, replenished each night by sunsets that break my heart, by the stamp of a deer's hoof in the twilight, by fierce owls with soft wings and claws of destruction, by cold that turns my breath into vapor that forms a cloud, then swirls away into the dark.

Desolation followed by consolation. Confession followed by inner cleansing. I entreat God in my prayers with the words from the psalmist, "Remember not our past sins; let your compassion be swift to meet us."

The day is being swallowed by the night; the cooler ing air magnifies a mouse's rustle in the tallgrass along th into a gunshot. My steps crackle loudly on the gravel road in the dusk. As I walk back to Parking Lot 25, twilight is beginning to lacquer the landscape in grays and blacks.

I reach for my keys and lean against the car, praying Compline's ending words: "Lord, you now have set your servant free to go in peace as you have promised."

Around me, the darkness is complete. But I'm forgiven.

Chapter Ten

Prairie Burn

The fire has no mercy. But it is not immortal.
When its fuel is consumed, it, too, will die.
—Annick Smith, Big Bluestem: Journey into the Tallgrass

Because nothing is mine in any real or permanent way, I have
(ultimately) nothing to fear from apparent losses in my life.
—Margaret Silf, Inner Compass

PAIN

In the late fall evenings, long after my family has gone to bed, I sit at the oak kitchen table, writing. Rubbing my eyes and yawning as the words begin to blur, I begin putting my journal and books away. It's then that I catch the slightest scent of the last red roses in the garden, blowing through the open windows.

Smelling roses, I become a child again. Clinging to my mother's hand, I am looking at a cold, hard-shelled silver casket in a dank mausoleum. Inside is my great-grandmother Laura's shrivelled frame. She's dead at eighty-six.

The casket is crowned by a spill of long-stemmed red roses.

When I open a florist's cooler and reach past red roses for a daisy bouquet to celebrate the birth of a friend's baby, or when I'm in a church for a December wedding and the vases overflow with scarlet blooms, the fragrance of sweet decay speaks to me of death. My husband, Jeff, never buys red roses for me for Valentine's Day or my birthday; he knows my aversion.

"Who doesn't love roses?" asks poet Mary Oliver. I don't. But like it or not, I'm stuck with them. When we moved to our house in the Chicago suburbs, our small backyard was mostly bare—no trees, a few hostas, dandelions. And roses. The one plant the elderly couple who had owned the house was fond of. Velvety red ones, drenched in smothering perfume.

An unwanted legacy.

My grandmother loves red roses, and she and my grandfather always had a few rosebushes. But now, a few hundred miles away from me, my grandfather lies curled up in a nursing-home bed. Once a robust man who could build a boat from nothing but lumber and nails, he now must be lifted from wheelchair to hospital bed by a sturdy young nurse. My grandmother, who could show me unerringly where the white violets bloomed each spring in the most hidden ravine hollows, can't remember any event much longer than a few minutes. She wanders through her empty house, wondering where my grandfather is, wondering why she is alone. Worried about death.

And portents of death are everywhere. As I drive to the prairie on cool autumn mornings, a murder of crows gloats by the highway. Sleek undertakers in shiny black suits, they descend on roadkill, cawing platitudes about mortality. Comical. Brutal.

Out on the prairie, the tallgrass is at its zenith, poised at the top of autumn and ready to plummet with the seasonal roller-coaster car down into winter. Decay is on the way. There's motion on the trail, and it's a pile of scat, vibrating with butterflies. A macabre feast. Rambling along the banks of Willoway Brook, I stumble over something half-buried in the yielding earth. Morning glory vines are knitting a polished raccoon skull to the soft ground, twining through the empty eye sockets, winding around the jawbone. The living embracing the dead.

The September grasses and forbs are gone to seed; wild white indigo pods emit a death rattle. *You sweep us away like a dream; we fade away suddenly like the grass. In the morning it is green and flourishes; in the evening it is dried up and withered.*

I shrink from death and all its symbols. Signs that this life is failing me, as it failed my grandmother and grandfather, as it fails everyone in the end. Cracks and fissures. I catch my reflection in a store window and see wrinkles lining the corners of my eyes. My hair falls out as I comb it, strewn all over the bathroom sink. I pick up a strand and hold it to the ht; the brown is draining to pure white.

Inserts in my shoes; underwires in my bra. I chat with a friend and begin to tell her the name of a book I recently read and find my mind utterly vacant. She's older than I am, and also short on memory. We both laugh hysterically.

And laugh. And laugh. Can we really laugh at death? *Oh death, where is your sting?* It's here, and God knows, it stings like a wasp. I'm walking the same path toward death my grandparents walk, although I'm years behind them. My spirit is moving closer to the landscape of heaven; my body is breaking down to return as dust to the landscape of earth.

This world as you see it is on its way out.

On the threshold of the sunshine's great decline into darkness, everything around me on the prairie looks broken. When I walk to my quiet spot, I see a desiccated toad smashed flat in the road; juices pressed out under a car tire, skin fused to asphalt, legs still in jump position.

The limestone ledge where I journal is littered with torn-off acorn caps and shattered shells. Leaves turn brown, then drop and molder under trees. Up in the black walnut tree, an eastern kingbird munches on a dragonfly. I take my binoculars out to get a closer look, and they snap in two in my hands.

Security is absent here. There's only brokenness. "What choice do we have in the grassland but to journey and to live in fear?" asks Richard Manning in *Grassland.* "How else can one see its fine and crushing beauty?" I'm afraid, I'm afraid, that the dark beauty of it all will crush me.

Our days on earth are like grass;
like wildflowers, we bloom and die.
The wind blows, and we are gone—
as though we had never been here.

In my backyard, the mulch pile is steaming, the wood chips and leaves breaking down, dying. The ancient willow next door splits in half on a peaceful, cloudless night and falls across the fence into my backyard, changing it into a landscape of destruction.

Dead limbs on the ground, dead snags in the woods. My garden is a mess of weeds. Corn has sprung up under the bird feeder, as well as stray sunflowers and something else . . . unidentifiable. There's a shriek in the backyard next door as a red-tailed hawk snatches a baby bunny from its mother, then tears it to bits. Mourning doves sift through fallen thistle seeds on my patio, keening a lament for the dead.

What a world, what a world . . .

Those who murmur platitudes about the beauty of nature should walk a trail with me one afternoon, observe my backyard, wade through Willoway Brook, and become acquainted with the world's messiness and terrors.

It makes starting over sound appealing.

Early each spring they set the Schulenberg Prairie on fire. It's usually late February or early March, when the dry grasses and plant material are a tinderbox waiting to go up in a roar of flames. "The grass is lush, spendthrift, doomed," observed the late poet Jane Kenyon, and so it is: nothing can save it from the fire that consumes everything in its path. It gulps down dead grass, sweeps away old flower stalks. In its wake it leaves a blackboard of ash, which waits for the sums of a new prairie year to be chalked upon it.

It's a seasonal cycle, people emulating nature, and one that brings enormous changes for the wildlife that inhabit the prairie. A chemotherapy of sorts, burning off that which would eventually destroy, making room for good things to come. As the flames warm the ground, the roots and seeds of wildflowers and grasses under the earth are stimulated to grow.

Walking out on the prairie after the burn in the early spring, I can only think of purification, loss, death. Everywhere is charred earth. There's a crunching under my hiking boots, and it's a deer mouse skeleton, scorched. Willoway Brook is choked with cinders.

What good could possibly come of this?

Still, life is cooking in a quiet sort of way. Grass blades looped like sewing needles emerge from the sooty ground, and prairie dropseed hummocks are haloed with blades of green hair. With the fields shorn of last year's tallgrass, hunting simplifies for the red-tailed hawk. He cruises above the sprouting landscape, thoughtfully scanning it for movement. Voles and mice are easy pickings. Killdeer embrace the scoured-clean prairie floor as the perfect place for a hastily constructed nest of a few sticks and stones, and suddenly, wherever I walk, I'm flushing the ring-necked birds.

Yet, my mouth tastes metallic with the bitterness of ashes.

I'm alone on the prairie most of this month. All the other visitors to the arboretum are over at the daffodil glade, exclaiming over the hundreds of thousands of blooming bulbs. A burned landscape holds little attraction.

However, "if our religion is something objective, then we must never avert our eyes from those elements in it which seem puzzling or repellent; for it will be precisely the puzzling or the repellent which conceals what we do not yet know and need to know," C.S. Lewis wrote in *The Weight of Glory*.

I struggle to accept faith without flinching. I try to pray through my fears, wondering if it's okay to be praying out of desperation. A frivolous question, because I know I will.

And, despite my prayers, death comes in the end. Joy followed by suffering. Vibrant flowers on the prairie crumple into decay, drop to the ground, are absorbed, and then shoot up again in the spring.

The same fall season that causes me to cling desperately to this life also hints of more to come; more than the landscape of earth we embrace with our five senses. *So teach us to number our days, that we may apply our hearts unto wisdom.*

I went out for Chinese food the other day with a friend, a Christian who has been a spiritual mentor for me. We'd been talking about someone whose life was a mess at the moment, and I mentioned I was praying about it. As we cracked open our fortune cookies, she remarked, "You know, I don't believe prayer really changes anything."

Her casual aside. I can't quit turning it over in my mind. It stands in sharp contrast to the words of my then six- and eight-year-old daughter and son, who had gone out exploring in the woods behind our house. I had spent a pleasant hour canning applesauce when they burst into the kitchen, flung their arms around me, and joyfully shouted, "Mom, we're okay!" I must have looked baffled—they weren't late, and I hadn't worried over anything more major than if I had enough jar lids to finish the canning. Dustin immediately explained, "We were lost and scared and couldn't find our way home, but we prayed to God and he showed us how to get back!" Their joy and confidence—a pure and holy thing.

I want my children's faith. But I've lost some joy and confidence. I've finally decided this: even if prayer doesn't change my circumstances—and I still believe it does—the act, the intentionality of my prayers changes me.

I don't choose suffering; I don't welcome pain. They've both cost me some of my joy and my confidence. But, I agree with the poet May Sarton, who called pain "the great teacher." After a bout of serious depression she wrote, "I do know that pain, which is usually caused by our relations with each other, has always been a means toward growth. . . . It is the sentimentalists who cannot bear to look at their pain, who wallow in it, and it is the cowards who simply shut it out by refusing to experience it."

Prairie fires. Death. I muse over these things again tonight as the fragrance of red roses pulls me outside. I select the sharpest knife from the silverware drawer, snap off the lights, and slip outside in the dark. The humidity on the windshield of the night sky is wiped to clearest visibility by autumn's arrival. A late-night breeze tickles my nose with its essence of burning firewood, damp earth, and the tang of apples fermenting. And roses.

The wind lifts my hair briefly; it's a breath of cold air, a refrigerator door opening and closing. Nearby, my tabby cat stalks through the dying sunflowers, and the tinkle of laughter and ice cubes in glasses wafts across the fence as the neighbors finish drinks on their screened-in porch before retiring.

Quietly, I pad barefoot through the damp unraked leaves to the garden and cut the last of the red roses. Five blooms in all. The petals of the largest are blackened at the borders, and the thorns prick my thumb.

Gingerly clasping them, I carry the bouquet into the kitchen. In the darkness, I arrange them in a blown-glass cobalt vase. I have brought them into warmth and tomorrow's light, where they will shatter more quickly than they would in the late September night's chill. A stark reminder of the world's temporal nature.

But the rootstocks of my red roses will remain dormant through the dark days of winter, until the spring rains rouse them from their torpor and warmth kindles their growth again. Under their snow blankets, they're alive and waiting. Through the long winter, however, all I will see is their brittle structure, seemingly dead.

When the last small fire on the prairie is extinguished, the prairie structure is all that is left. The bur oaks, whose bark was created to tolerate the hot fire, endure. The paths that wind through the upper and lower fields stand out in bold relief against the black ground. The bridges that link the paths still stand, spanning Willoway Brook. The prairie is a blank slate, ready for writing.

After a period of suffering, I am completely spent. Laid waste. Often pain sweeps through me like flames over the prairie, leaving nothing but scorched earth. I'm pared down to the core; all I counted on, everything I relied on, the people I leaned on, the familiar, are seemingly gone in a few short hours. I'm a blank slate.

It is then that I hold fast to these words from Hugh of Balma: "At length the whole combustible material is purged of its own nature and passes into the similitude and property of fire. Then the din is hushed, and the voracious fire, having subdued all and brought all into its own likeness, composes itself to a high peace and silence, finding nothing more that is alien or opposed to itself."

Letting go of control as much as I can, I offer my loss of joy and confidence to God as prayer, waiting for peace and silence. *Lord have mercy. Christ have mercy.* Sometimes this prayer is the most important of my day, especially if I am at the bottom of a cycle of depression and can barely form a sentence . . . a particularly difficult place to be if your livelihood is writing.

When I pray for mercy, I am caught up with the hawk, spiraling higher and higher in an updraft, held by a power that is not of my doing, something untamed and wild. A force that moves me beyond words, through despondency, and into a higher presence. It's relinquishment of all control, and surrender to faith.

Lord have mercy. Christ have mercy.

CHAPTER ELEVEN

Sandhill Cranes

A bird does not sing because it has an answer.
It sings because it has a song.

—CHINESE PROVERB

Whoever sings, prays twice.

—ST. AUGUSTINE

JOY

~~~~~~~~

*T*he tree is trimmed, the packages are wrapped, and a last flurry of shopping and behind-the-doors activity is in process. Christmas Eve. I take advantage of my family's busyness to slip out and spend an hour on the prairie, still open despite the holiday until five o'clock. Amazingly, Jack, who is the lone arboretum employee on the premises and working the entry gate, has a smile and a chirpy "Merry Christmas" for me as I stop in at the gatehouse. I feel considerably cheered.

Which is welcome. With age has come a loss of much of the joy I used to have about Christmas. I'm often depressed rather than anticipatory, stressed rather than excited, and anxious about the money we spend rather than focused on what's worthy of celebration. The Christmas season invites the blues.

Out on the prairie, the limestone ledge is frosted four inches thick with white layers of icing. I follow the trails left by deer and coyote, noting where the coyote prints cross the wooden bridge and meet the deer tracks. The coyote has peed at the intersection, marking his territory, leaving a lemonade stain.

In the back field by the outbuilding, I spot a young buck wading through a gaggle of Canada geese. He watches me warily, motionless. His brown coat is glossy in the sunshine. Deciding I'm harmless, he noses through the snow to pull at the half-frozen grasses. Deer eat the rarest prairie flora's tender blooms during the warmer seasons, but I can't help loving the sight of him browsing in the sunshine.

I walk through drifts. Blue shadows sweep out in front of me, trees shadowed and elongated in cobalt. Small soft hollows are puddled with azure. Indigo pours into the squirrel's paired footprints, evenly spaced across the trail, linking the trees. Mouse tracks double-stitch the landscape's hem.

Sun shines high in an aluminum sky. I step carefully, white powder spilling into my boot tops, crusting my jeans up to the knees. Before I know it I'm singing; the notes spill from my mouth into vapor wisps that hang for a moment in the cold clear day, then rise and mingle into the clouds that coast through the blue sky overhead. Warbled song fragments.

I finish walking my regular loop, and then I ease my way into the snow piled on the limestone ledge and unscrew my thermos lid. The peppermint tea is hot, too hot, and I burn my lips. Some of the cold is taken away by the fiery liquid. Through my jeans, my legs freeze, then go numb.

Willoway Brook is slick with ice, its surface crazed with a million jagged crackles. Fired with a chill glaze, it is immobile and brittle, although open expanses show greenish-black icy depths. A splash echoes in the distance. The quiet is underscored with the continuous sound of water moving under the ice.

Foxtail grasses poke out of embankments, sporting frost mustaches. Canada thistle skeletons are silhouetted against the wintry background. The wind bends grass tips down into the snow, scribbling indecipherable messages. Breezes polish the prairie's surface, smoothing out the rough spots.

In the air currents overhead, a red-tailed hawk circles and shrieks. A black-capped chickadee perches on a nearby branch and asks, "See me-me-me-me-me? See me-me-me-me-me?" I do.

I see other birds as well, decked out like clergymen in their winter whites and blacks and grays. Woodpecker, woodpecker, junco, goose. Nuthatch, mallard, mallard, goose. The conventional December line-up. A gash of red—a cardinal colors outside the lines. Their notes stamp the landscape with song.

The naked trees stretch their limbs, their shadows marked in blue on the earth's white skin, veining it with cerulean. The sky reverses the landscape: overhead a burnished blue marbled with meringue; underneath the earth bleached white and shadowed with blue.

The blues. I've had them, I've got them, but they are leaving me in this place. "When God's spirit moves, he leaves singing in his wake," observes musician Michael Card. The monks knew this with their chanting. Prayer and music are tightly knit together; one is a springboard for the other. The inner well of joy created by prayer bubbles up and overflows, flooding the soul with song.

I leave my thermos and hip pack on the ledge and walk up the trail. Throwing myself into a snowbank, I make snow angels along the iced tallgrass. I sing with the psalmist, "I've thrown myself headlong into your arms. I'm celebrating your rescue. I'm singing at the top of my lungs, I'm so full of answered prayers."

It's clouding up, and I sit on the ledge for a few me moments before gathering my thermos and hip pa leave. The sun is a white-hot dime burning a hole through the clouds, which swirl, then smother the sun again, darkening the sky. Without sunlight the creek loses its shimmer, becomes flat metal. Snowflakes fall softly. My edges also soften, and I melt into the landscape. In a frozen hour, I will be submerged in it, indistinguishable in my black and brown coat, my dark hair blending into the scenery, snow blurring my profile. Covered in white.

The cold December light is beginning to fade, and the clouds move in earnestly now. Snow is falling more thickly. Time to leave. I snowplow a path back down the trail with my boots. Singing under my breath.

I'm not singing alone. Another chant begins far away, then intensifies. Eerie, high-pitched music. Coming from over my head. Closer.

A flurry of wings and a rush of sound. Louder. Louder. A flock of sandhill cranes, stopping off on their journey south. "You're late!" I whisper, scarcely daring to believe.

I've never been this close to so many. They shouldn't be ⸱. The winter is well under way, but doubtless the unsea-

ᴸy warm weather of early December has caused them to

linger in their northern fields. They hover over Willoway Brook in a winged flurry.

An unexpected epiphany.

In the earliest world legends, cranes have a near-sacred place as messengers. Peter Matthiessen writes that heaven-bound ancients are commonly depicted riding on a crane; and these cranes, with their astonishing appearance, seem celestial, other-worldly. I count them until I reach sixty, then give up and listen, their piercing cries raising a supernatural sound to the heavens.

A wonder.

They slowly drop from the sky, settling in for the night. Ready to usher in Christmas morning and, with it, good tidings.

Of great joy.

Chapter Twelve

Twilight

To make a prairie it takes a clover and one bee,
One clover, and a bee,
And revery.
The revery alone will do
If bees are few.
—Emily Dickinson

Surely, it is your business, so far as you may, to express in
action something of the real character of that universe within
which you now know yourself to live?
—Evelyn Underhill, Practical Mysticism

CREATIVITY

꧁꧂

$\mathcal{A}$s the autumn days grow shorter on the prairie, it's the narrow slivers of time between light and darkness that are endlessly fascinating in their elusiveness. I deliberately linger on my walks, waiting for that moment when day passes the baton to night.

Across the two-track from the limestone ledge where I wait, the bunnies move noiselessly in the grassy hollow. They're foraging for dinner under the gathering gloom's cover. One . . . two . . . three. . . . Soft brown ears barely show above the grasses as they sit back on their haunches, sniffing the air for predators. Above them the wind finger-paints with the clouds, swirling in more purples, grays, and blacks. In the west, violet clouds are massing, loaded with liquid and advancing. Mars, shining red and warrior-like, plays tag with the full moon, which rides the waves of the darkening sky.

As the last light turns the midges rising off Willoway Brook into flying sequins, nighthawks and barn swallows mingle in the evening air, sieving it for insects. Indigo buntings murmur to each other from the cottonwood trees, and a great horned owl purrs in the woods that fringe the prairie. Prairie dropseed's hot buttered popcorn smell infuses the air along the path as the first mosquito of the night pinches my bare arm. I lie full length on the limestone ledge, relishing the coolness of the rock against my cheek.

The sun is setting into the dark clouds, backlighting the landscape, and the temperature falls. Twilight begins.

That trick of the light. It is what drives me to paint, even though I do it poorly, but you can come closer to capturing the light through brushstrokes than you ever could do with a camera. The difficulty is, even when you get the light's angle and the colors right with paints, the results look overdone. It's a problem with autumn in general: all those contrasts of scarlet, lemon, and that odd burnished metal color of sky, with a black crow inking itself across it. It's also a quandary with the fall landscape at dusk in particular, with angles of luminescence that change by the second. You can see why Monet kept painting the wheat stacks to explore the changes of the light.

The New England asters showcase the light-change effect, with their golden eyes fringed in deep purple glowing against the bleached-out backdrop of Indian grass right before sunset. The backlighting as the sun drops makes each blade, each petal, each leaf incandescent. At the Schulenberg Prairie, the Indian-grass plumes brighten right as the sun falls below the earth's horizon. The foamy seed heads catch the sun's final rays, and the warm rose violet of the sky is reflected in the tawny warm colors of the tallgrass.

You can capture twilight to some extent with words, which is why I keep scribbling about it in my journal. I later read over the entries, and certain prairie scenes are vividly conjured up for me. Still, the words leave me vaguely dissatisfied.

Twilight also influences the creative arrangements in my garden. Tonight the white asters—*aster simplex*—are a thousand tiny stars; anything white is luminous in last light. I used to have a white garden for this reason, so I could sit outside at dusk and watch it glow in the evening right as the sun fell below the horizon. In my backyard, I still choose white flowers, shuffle them around to get the best effects, looking for the most brilliant blooms that will communicate beauty at dusk.

The Great Lakes Ojibwa Indians must have felt an artistic desire to communicate when they painted pictographs on the cliffs along Lake Superior's shores. Some of their images were later covered with graffiti, and the disparity was notable. "There is a fundamental difference between aboriginal marks on stone and pioneer inscriptions, based on the separate philosophical relationships to the land. . . . One regarded land as a spiritual source of identity, the other saw land as property," observes anthropologist Thor Conway in *Painted Dreams.* He also notes, "The soul speaks in the language of images and symbols."

Our soul longs to speak. Isn't this offering-up of our creativity a prayer in itself? Our soul speaking in paint, in words, in landscape? An attempt to open a window between us and something greater than ourselves that we dimly perceive, try to express?

Twilight is mystery, a bit of the subconscious. Primitive. There's slight anxiety as the sun slips from sight. Will it return to bathe the world in light again?

The creative muse is also elusive. I often sit with my journal open, empty of words. I stare at the empty canvas, tentative, paralyzed. Flowers in my garden mysteriously die, pop up in unexpected places, or fail to appear in the spring, and I despair of ever making the garden in my head appear in my backyard. "In creating, the only hard thing is to begin: a grass blade's no easier to make than an oak," wrote James Russell Lowell. I find a thousand different reasons to put off beginning a creative project, especially when I know my best efforts will fall far short of what I envision.

But the urge to create remains.

This urge was understood by the mystic Evelyn Underhill, who knew the desire to pour out our creativity to God:

> *Artists, aware of a more vivid and more beautiful world than other men, are always driven by their love and enthusiasm to attempt the expression, the bringing into manifestation of those deeper significances of form, sound, rhythm, which they have been able to apprehend: and in doing this, they taste deeper and deeper truths, make ever closer unions with the Real. For them, the duty of creation is tightly bound up with the gift of love. In their passionate outflowing to the universe which offers itself under one of its many aspects to their adoration, that other-worldly fruition of beauty is always followed, balanced, completed, by a this-world impulse to creation: a desire to fix within the time*

order, and share with other men, the vision by which they were possessed.

This fall crepuscular light is a marvel by itself; occasionally I see wonder upon wonder. One evening as I walk the two-track, a sun halo appears. It's a rainbow-hued ring that fills the sky, with the bottom curve dropping out below the earth to the west. Two "sundogs"—little bright spots of rainbow-colored light on the halo's sides—are clearly visible, riding the edges. Sun halos form when sunshine passes through ice crystals in cirrostratus clouds, and they often foretell rain or snow.

These are fairly common. Why haven't I noticed them before? What else have I failed to pay attention to? The prairie sky gives me an almost panoramic view, a perspective difficult to have elsewhere in the Chicago suburbs.

Impossible to recreate. Extravagant. My artistic efforts to mirror the landscape around me always leave me vexed, yet determined to try again.

Darkness vacuums up the prairie's shadows, and Willoway Brook turns black. Dawn has cycled to twilight. Having this desire to connect with my creator, I'll pray with my brushstrokes, worship with my words, plant white asters in my garden.

And always, walk the prairie at sunset.

Chapter Thirteen

Conservationists

I believe a leaf of grass is no less than the journeywork of the stars.

—Walt Whitman, "Song of Myself"

The soul's profit, then, consists not in thinking much, but in loving much.

—Teresa of Avila, The Interior Castle

MENTORS

$\mathcal{T}$oday I drive 45 minutes southwest of the arboretum to spend the morning with Ray Schulenberg, the eighty-some-thing-year-old father of the prairie that is his namesake. I first met him when he addressed a fundraiser for the new prairie visitors' center, and I immediately fell for his delightful sense of humor, unassertiveness, and refusal to say what was expected. As the keynote speaker for the fundraiser, he expressed some concerns about the new construction: "I sure hope they don't widen the paths and cause us to lose more native plants!" His passion for the prairie permeated everything he said.

When my older prairie volunteer friends talk about Ray, they use a reverential tone much like the one my church friends use when speaking of the Almighty. His way of describing plants he approves of, "the rare and beautiful prairie gentian," in contrast to those of which he disap-proves, "the hated and vicious multiflora rose," is legendary. Not only was Ray instrumental in reconstructing the Schulenberg Prairie, he also has instilled a love of all things prairie in legions of those he has come in contact with.

My native-plant garden group, "The Wild Ones," has arranged a morning at Ray's friend Dave Kropp's house and land, where Ray now lives. Dave and Ray greet us with a warm hello and a handshake, and then Ray takes a little group on an hour-long walk through the three-and-a-half-acre prairie planting.

Ray is, by his own admission, "a little crippled up," doubtless from the backbreaking work establishing the prairie that bears his name. Although he leans on his cane, he sets a pretty brisk pace through the tallgrass. Occasionally he uses his cane to point out a particularly interesting specimen: the glade mallow, a nice stand of big bluestem, or the red-winged blackbird's perfectly formed nest in a low-spreading wild indigo plant.

Latin names spill off his tongue, and Ray knows every animal, plant, butterfly, and tree on the property. He's also quick to point out that "prairie plantings"—like this one and the one with his name on it at the arboretum—are lovely, but not as dazzling as "prairie remnants"—native prairie parcels that survived the plow and modern construction ravages. "It's hard to establish small, early spring flowers in prairie plantings," Ray says. "Remnants have them, but our artificial plantings usually don't." He looks at the oldest section of the prairie planting we're observing and sighs. "This is close to what it looked like before the honkies came to Illinois."

Mentors point the way for me in learning about both nature and prayer. In nature knowledge, a prairie ecology instructor at the local college unlocked many landscape secrets for me, and my prairie volunteer group has several veteran members who patiently answer my endless questions. "The Wild Ones" garden group does a monthly slide-show and lecture series about native plants that adds more informational nuggets to my growing prairie lexicon. And, should an alien plant rear its head in my backyard prairie patch, my native-plant savvy neighbors, Gerould and Margaret Wilhelm and their son Dave, are always willing to drop what they are doing and help me put a name to what I see.

The word *mentor* means trusted adviser. When I respect someone, I pay attention to what he or she teaches. I'm only meeting Ray for the second time, but I know his work because I'm out on the prairie every day. It's given me respect for the one who orchestrated its beauty. When Ray speaks, I listen.

As Ray talks to us about prairie restorations and prairie reconstruction, he says he has two goals for a prairie planting—

make it diverse, and keep it weed free. "The Good Book says that 'the weeds you will have with you always,' " he says, then laughs. "Okay, maybe it doesn't exactly say that."

His prairie philosophy translates well for my spiritual life and for my learning from "the Good Book. "

I'm surrounding myself with eclectic mentors who all teach me a little bit about prayer. One mentor is a business colleague who prays regularly at certain times of the day. If she's in a group or a meeting, she excuses herself for a few minutes and disappears. Her commitment to pray supersedes her business commitments.

Another woman I admire runs a publishing house where all incoming phone calls are answered by machine during times when the employees break for prayer. I have friends whose lives silently speak commitment to me, although I never see them actually pray—they do so in private. Prayer creates a quiet center their lives revolve around, reflected in the way they treat the *barista* at the coffee shop, how they speak to their spouses, or the goals they aspire to attain. Their prayers are not about what they *say;* they are about what they *do*. Their lives teach me more about prayer than public and often showy verbal petitions and praises.

Not to say I don't learn from those who pray out loud. The table prayers of my grandfather envelop my childhood memories in a beautiful mist of comfort and security. When my family holds hands around the table and prays together before a meal, I find in my children's simple words the wholehearted trust I sometimes lack. Praying the Lord's Prayer together as a church community reminds me what I long for in prayer, yet can't attain without support.

True mentors teach me through their examples, throw cold water on my complacency, and stimulate me to continue learning more about the planet I live on and the world that's still to come. As I absorb from them new ideas about prayer, I make discoveries about myself. I avoid people who "yes" me to death. My dearest friends come alongside me, help keep me on track, and aren't afraid to be tough about it.

As a writer who works odd and solitary hours, I'm often tempted to go it alone, to do everything myself. I lose my perspective and many times find myself discouraged. My prayers, like my prairie knowledge, are not built on learning solo. Mentors show me the way.

Chapter Fourteen

After the Rain

It began in mystery, and it will end in mystery, but what a
savage and beautiful country lies in between.

—DIANE ACKERMAN, A Natural History of the Senses

Metaphorical images can bring us to God,
but once we stand face to face with God's imageless glory,
we realize the impoverishment of all imagination.

—BELDEN LANE, The Solace of Fierce Landscapes

MYSTERY

$\mathcal{A}$ theology professor I know kept hearing me rave about the Schulenberg Prairie, its myriad grasses, its floral diversity, the glorious changing of its seasons, until he was likely sick unto death of the conversation. Finally he took an afternoon off and went out to see the prairie for himself. The next time he saw me, he was genuinely mystified. "Weeds, Cindy," he said, scratching his head. "It's nothing but weeds."

To me, *theology* seems like weeds.

I'm endlessly captivated by the fluctuating seasons on the prairie, but I've come to realize that not everyone sees this landscape as I do. Summer is closing up shop, and the prairie is slipping into a season of slow decline. Autumn is ready to tap me on the shoulder at any moment, and I keep looking behind me, not wanting to be caught off guard. Walnut leaves mixed with bright yellow goldfinches are thrown like glitter through the air, and I'm often confused by which is which until the finch pulls itself out of a dive and twitters back to cruising altitude, or the leaf slips down to the prairie floor.

I find the prairie a kinetic, energetic, ever-shifting kaleidoscope. Others find it nothing but weeds. But as garden writer Henry Mitchell said, that's for folks who "don't see much when they look."

What I don't comprehend can leave me certain it is not worth my time, or it can invite me to investigate and understand. My ignorance can let me go on my way, dismissing what I don't immediately grasp, or I can let the unknown draw me in until I dimly sense what is veiled. It's easy to live life in a fog and lose my awe, my amazement for what each season sets in motion. I could forfeit that very journal of creation that will teach me, if I let it, what will save me; exchanging it for things that give only passing gratification, leaving me empty and yearning for something more.

The prairie paths that once confounded me with their strangeness have long since grown routine; the landscape has unveiled secrets for me as I examined it from unusual perspectives. The earth has rotated upon her axis again and again, spinning through space, and the sun has risen and set on a thousand different stories enacted in the tallgrass since I took the first step on my journey of learning to pray.

This evening on the prairie, the world is newly washed, post-storm fresh after a long drought. Swallows and nighthawks are exulting in the cooler air, swooping and darting to catch the insects rising off Willoway Brook. The tallgrass is alive with butterflies, dragonflies, grasshoppers, and birds, weaving in and out.

The early fall landscape has a skein of Queen Anne's lace crocheted into it. Buttery-yellow false sunflowers are dabbed around the wooden bridge, and there's a depression where a deer has made its bed in the tallgrass—a moist mattress of smashed bottle gentians, with prairie dropseed for a pillow. The summer's drought left the prairie lightly singed; now the rain has softened the *Silphiums'* brittle edges and polished the cracked earth to a smooth, creamy luster. Tall cup plants have collected the night's shower in their clasping leaves, and the goldfinches perch on their thick stems, disappearing into the sandpapery chalices to sip and to splash.

My life is slowly coming to revolve around prayer. I'm beginning to understand what Evelyn Underhill was trying to say when she used St. Teresa's well-known image: "You have been watering the garden of your spirit by hand; a poor and laborious method, yet one in which there is a definite relation between effort and result. But now the watering-can is taken from you, and you must depend upon the rain: more generous, more fruitful, than anything which your own efforts could manage, but in its incalculable visitations, utterly beyond your control."

I was drought-crisped, and now I'm rain-reliant. Accepting what comes, then offering it back. Letting go of control. Learning this thing called prayer.

Nothing is new under the sun, says the book of Ecclesiastes, yet this planet seethes with things I haven't seen, heard, or understood. I see the sum of the whole but often fail to appreciate its parts. I see, and yet I don't see. I look at Willoway Brook and observe the water, some trailing plants, the gravel at the bottom, a few fish. When I take out my little magnifying glass and look up close, twirling my fingers through the water, I stir up a squirming, floating melee of minutiae, a universe swimming inches from my nose. They are part of the prairie's structure, building blocks of the world.

In finding structure for my prayers, I've found a place of rest where growth is possible in the fullest sense. It's a paradox, that discipline leads to freedom—but as this prayer framework becomes a solid part of my faith, I find that what believers throughout the centuries have known is also true for me. The structure, the habits of a life of prayer are giving me a spiritual freedom I've never had.

The pasture thistles spike seven feet tall, blooming purple, their flowers bursting from their pineapple-like swollen bases and then turning to pliable down puffs. Around me, the goldfinches are nesting. They've waited all summer until these thorny thistles exploded in soft blossoms, which they'll use to line their nests. Living in the rhythm of the landscape, taking up their appointed places in the universe's structure as the seasons turn.

I'm quiet, listening to them fly back and forth. *Be still and know.*

Willoway Brook winds a diamond necklace through the tallgrass, reflecting the sunlight's last glimmer. An early full moon rises in the east to hang breathless over the tips of the larches. My shadow lengthens as the sun slides toward the horizon and twilight dims the sky.

The land is teaching me. Prayer is opening my eyes to things I didn't know. I have a covenant with both—to maintain a habit of being there, of showing up to learn from exterior and interior landscapes.

To learn a particular landscape takes more than a cursory walk-through, a token look-see. It means investing myself in it and letting it invade me, letting it in under my skin. To see it in all seasons: heat and snow, sun and rain, wind and calms. I assimilate the prairie's essence: wade in the brook, taste the mountain mint, run fingers through the silky grasses.

My interior landscape is slowly unfolding as I establish a habit of *being there*: experimenting with waiting, with confession, with singing, with learning from the community around me, and with reading the words of those who have gone before me.

Yet with all my observing, walking and listening, waiting and naming, much remains elusive. I've found that with the prairie and in prayer, the more I scribble in my journal and find names for what I see and understand, the greater the chasm of mystery becomes. The more questions I ask.

"The world does not become less 'unknown' in the proportion to the increase of our knowledge about it. . . . Our experience of the world involves us in a mystery which can be intelligible to us only as mystery," wrote Henry Bugbee. "The more we experience depth, the more we participate in mystery intelligible to us only as such."

As the shadows lengthen and the sun sets in a glowing red fireball, I am content with my journey. It's not over, but my feet are firmly on the path now, and I'm not turning aside. I know the places of rest. I anticipate what is still to be learned and to be grasped, and I make my peace with the mystery of the ungraspable God who created the landscape that connects me to him.

I lie down in the tallgrass and let it absorb me into the landscape. The dirt beneath me is spongy and soft; the little bluestem crayons the surrounding grasses with platinum. The prairie is remaking me; prayer is transforming me. By learning the rhythms of the landscape, I'm learning the rhythms of my soul. I will follow these paths until I finally walk into the embrace of the eternal.

The landscape to come.

Grass is where I began my journey,
and in grass I will end it.

—ANNICK SMITH,
Big Bluestem: Journey into the Tallgrass

NOTES

EPIGRAPH

Mary Oliver, "The Summer Day," *House of Light* (Boston: Beacon Press, 1990), 94.

INTRODUCTION
Exploring Interior and Exterior Landscapes

p. xv. N. Scott Momaday, *The Way to the Rainy Mountain* (Albuquerque: New Mexico: University of New Mexico Press, 2001), 83.

CHAPTER ONE
Mud Season: Despair

p. 2. Doug Ladd, *Tallgrass Prairie Wildflowers: A Field Guide* (Helena, Montana: Falcon Publishing, Inc. 1995), 6, quoting Eliza Steele, *Summer Journey in the West.* Steele was writing about what she observed in 1840 near Joliet, Illinois, about 30 miles south of the present-day Schulenberg Prairie.

p. 2. Wayne Muller, *Sabbath: Finding Rest, Renewal, and Delight in our Busy Lives* (New York: Random House Inc., Bantam Books, 1999), 182.

p. 8. Anne Lamott, *Traveling Mercies* (New York: Random House, Inc., Anchor Books/Pantheon Books, 1999), 82.

p. 8. Thomas Merton, *The Sign of Jonas* (New York: Harcourt Brace Jovanovich, 1979), 236.

p. 8. Shirley Shirley, *Restoring the Tallgrass Prairie: An Illustrated Manual for Iowa and the Upper Midwest* (Iowa City, Iowa: University of Iowa Press, 1994), ix.

p. 9. Joel Greenberg, *A Natural History of the Chicago Region* (Chicago, Illinois: University of Chicago Press, 2002), 465, notes that the Schulenberg Prairie is the second reconstruction nationwide, and the first in the Chicago region.

p. 9. John Madson in *Where the Sky Began: Land of the Tallgrass Prairie* (Ames, Iowa: Iowa State University Press, 1982, 1995), 284, quoting Mark Hall, the primary restorationist of the prairie in Alton, Illinois, in Gordon Moore Park.

p. 10. Richard Manning, *Grassland: The History, Biology, Politics, and Promise of the American Prairie* (New York: Penguin), 259, 260.

p. 11. Barry Lopez, *Arctic Dreams* (New York: Scribner and Sons, 1986), 411.

CHAPTER TWO
Nighthawks: Waiting

p. 12. John Madson, *Tallgrass Prairie* (Helena and Billings, Montana: Falcon Press Publishing Co., Inc.), 15, quoting William A. Quayle, *The Prairie and the Sea*.

p. 12. Carlo Carretto, *The God Who Comes,* quoted in *A Guide to Prayer for Ministers & Other Servants,* ed. Reuben Job and Norman Shawchuck (Nashville, Tennessee: Upper Room Books, 1990), 15.

p. 16. Anne Morrow Lindbergh, *Gift from the Sea* (New York: Random House, Inc., Pantheon Books, 1955/1991), 36.

p. 20. John Wesley, as quoted in *A Guide to Prayer for Ministers & Other Servants,* ed. Reuben Job and Norman Shawchuck (Nashville, Tennessee: Upper Room Books, 1990), 34.

p. 21. Annie Dillard, *Pilgrim at Tinker Creek* (New York: Harper and Row, 1974), 218.

CHAPTER THREE
High Winds: Spirit

p. 24. Donald Culross Peattie, *Weather: A Naturalist's Journal* (Mahons Point, Australia: Time Life Books, The Nature Company, Weldon Owen Pty Ltd., 1996).

p. 24. Romans 8, *The Message*, Eugene Peterson (Colorado Springs, Colorado: NavPress, 1995).

p. 29. Joel 2:28–29, *New Living Translation* (Wheaton, Illinois: Tyndale House Publishers, Inc., 1996).

CHAPTER FOUR
Dragonflies: Attention

p. 32. Thanks to the poet Mary Oliver for her beautiful poetry and prose on paying attention that inspired this chapter.

p. 32. Diane Ackerman, *A Natural History of the Senses* (New York: Random House, Inc., Vintage Books, 1990), 305.

p. 32. *A Guide to Prayer for Ministers & Other Servants,* ed. Reuben Job and Norman Shawchuck (Nashville, Tennessee: Upper Room Books, 1990), quoting John H. Westerhoff III and John D. Eusden from *The Spiritual Life.*

p. 35. The term "movable feast" comes from the title of Ernest Hemingway's classic *A Moveable Feast* (New York: Touchstone Books, 1996).

CHAPTER FIVE
New Paths: Change

p. 40. Terry Tempest Williams, *Red: Passion and Patience in the Desert* (New York: Random House, Inc., Pantheon Books, 2001), 24.

p. 40. Belden C. Lane, *The Solace of Fierce Landscapes: Exploring Desert and Mountain Spirituality* (New York: Oxford University Press, 1998), 117.

p. 50. Willa Cather, *Death Comes for the Archbishop* (New York: Random House, Inc., Vintage House Classics, 1927), 50.

p. 51. Robert M. Hamma, *Earth's Echo: Sacred Encounters With Nature* (Notre Dame, Indiana: Sorin Books, 2002), 86.

CHAPTER SIX
Monarchs: Longings

p. 52. Stephen Rowe and David Lubbers, *Abiding: Landscape of the Senses* (Grand Rapids, Michigan: Eerdmans, 1998), 19.

p. 52. Robert Benson, *Venite* (New York: Penguin Putnam Inc., Jeremy P. Tarcher/ Putnam, 2000), 194.

p. 53. Sue Halpern, *Four Wings and a Prayer: Caught in the Mystery of the Monarch Butterfly* (New York: Random House, Inc., Pantheon Books, 2001), 11, 12.

p. 54. Scott Weidensaul, *Living on the Wind: Across the Hemisphere with Migratory Birds* (New York: Farrar, Straus and Giroux, North Point Press, 1999), 82.

p. 57. Gretel Ehrlich, *The Solace of Open Spaces* (New York: Penguin Books, 1986), 103.

p. 58. Ken Gire, *The Gift of Remembrance* (Grand Rapids, Michigan: Zondervan Publishing House, 1990), 3, quoting a Jewish proverb.

p. 58. Diane Ackerman, *Natural History of the Senses* (New York: Random House Inc., Vintage Books, 1990), 204.

p. 59. Terry Tempest Williams, *Refuge* (New York: Random House Inc., Pantheon Books, 1991), 4.

p. 60. Gretel Ehrlich, *This Cold Heaven: Seven Seasons in Greenland* (New York: Random House Inc., Pantheon Books, 2001), 111. Ehrlich asks Stephen Hawkins's unanswerable question: "Is it possible to remember the future?"

p. 60. C.S. Lewis, *The Voyage of the Dawn Treader,* from The Chronicles of Narnia (New York: HarperCollins, 1952, renewed 1980), 234–244.

CHAPTER SEVEN
Field Guides: Learning

p. 62. Mary Blocksma, *Naming Nature: 365 Days to Natural Literacy* (New York: Penguin Books, USA, Viking Penguin, 1992), xi, xii.

p. 62. C.S. Lewis. This quote seems to be more anecdotal, than anything—in the movie *Shadowlands,* Anthony Hopkins, who plays Lewis, uses this line; and the quote itself pops up all over attributed to Lewis—I even have it on a greeting card pinned up on my bulletin board over my desk! No one, however, seems to attribute it to any specific book.

p. 64. Donald and Lillian Stokes, *Stokes Field Guide to Birds, Eastern Region* (Boston: Little, Brown and Company, 1996).

p. 65. *National Geographic Field Guide to the Birds of North America* (Washington, D.C.: National Geographic, 1999).

p. 65. Kenn Kaufman, *Birds of North America* (New York: Houghton Mifflin, Hillstar Editions, 2000).

p. 66. Peter Slater, Pat Slater, Raoul Slater, *The Slater Field Guide to Australian Birds* (Australia: Landsdowne, 2000).

p. 66. David Allen Sibley, illustrator; Chris Elphick, John B. Dunning, Jr., David Allen Sibley, editors, *The Sibley Guide to Bird Life & Behavior* (New York: Alfred A. Knopf, 2001).

p. 66. In his magisterial work, *Living on the Wind: Across the Hemisphere with Migratory Birds* (see Chapter 6 notes), Scott Weinensaul also compares how different naturalists and guide books intepret the call of the sandhill crane. As he so wisely notes (p. 280), "I suppose I am not the only one who has thrown up his hands in defeat." Amen.

p. 69. *The Book of Common Prayer* (New York: HarperCollins, Seabury Press, 1991).

p. 70. Robert Benson, *Venite* (New York: Penguin Putnam, Inc., Jeremy P. Tarcher/Putnam, 2000).

p. 70. Phyllis Tickle, *The Divine Hours: Springtime, Summertime, Autumn/Winter,* 3 vols. (New York: Doubleday, 2000, 2001).

p. 71. Wayne Muller, *Sabbath: Finding Rest, Renewal, and Delight in Our Busy Lives* (New York: Bantam Books, 1999).

p. 72. "Red Book," *A Guide to Prayer for All God's People,* ed. Rueben Job and Norman Shawchuck (Nashville, Tennessee: Upper Room Books, 1990).

p. 72. "Blue Book," *A Guide to Prayer for Ministers and Other Servants,* ed. Reuben Job and Norman Shawchuck (Nashville, Tennessee: Upper Room Books, 1990).

p. 72. Lorraine Kisly, ed., *Watch and Pray: Christian Teachings on the Practice of Prayer* (New York: Random House, Inc., Crown Publishing Group, Bell Tower, 2002).

p. 72. St. Teresa of Avila, *The Interior Castle*, as quoted in *A Guide to Prayer for Ministers and Other Servants*, ed. Reuben Job and Norman Shawchuck, (Nashville: Upper Room Books, 1990), 27.

p. 74. Kathleen Norris, *The Cloister Walk* (New York: G.P. Putnam & Sons, Riverhead, 1996).

p. 74. Phyllis Tickle, *The Shaping of A Life: A Spiritual Landscape* (New York: Doubleday, 2001).

p. 74. Robert Benson, *Living Prayer* (New York: Jeremy P. Tarcher/Putnam, 1998).

p. 75. Thomas Merton, *The Sign of Jonas* (New York: Harcourt Brace Jovanovich, 1979), 102.

CHAPTER EIGHT
Pulling Weeds: Community

p. 78. Aldo Leopold, *Sand County Almanac* (New York: Oxford University Press, 1949), viii.

p. 78. Lorraine Kisly, ed., *Watch and Pray: Christian Teachings on the Practice of Prayer* (New York: Random House, Inc., Crown Publishing Group, Bell Tower, 2002), 194, 195, quoting from the general instruction of the Catholic *The Liturgy of the Hours.*

p. 84. Some of the information on sweet clover, *Melilotus alba,* is from *All About Weeds* by Edwin Rollin Spencer (New York: Dover, 1974), 135, 136, and Joel Greenberg's *A Natural History of the Chicago Region* (Chicago, Illinois: University of Chicago Press, 2002), 61.

p. 87. William Bryant Logan, *Dirt: The Ecstatic Skin of the Earth* (New York: Riverhead Books, published by The Berkley Publishing Group, 1995), 74.

CHAPTER NINE
Compass Plants: Confession

p. 90. John James Ingalls, "In Praise of Blue Grass," from *Grass: The Yearbook of Agriculture* (Washington, D.C.: USDA, 1948), as reprinted from the Web site [http://turfgrass.com/ingalls/].

p. 90. Kathleen Norris, *The Cloister Walk* (New York: G.P. Putnam & Sons, Riverhead, 1996), 165.

p. 93. Information about the compass plant and its weevil was influenced by information given me by Craig Johnson, Director of External affairs and manager of the Schulenberg Prairie, the Morton Arboretum, Lisle, Illinois, and research information done by John F. Tooker, graduate student, Department of Entomology, University of

Illinois at Urbana-Champaign, found online at [www.life.uiuc.edu/hanks/tooker/]. Other information about the compass plant was gleaned from Shirley Shirley's *Restoring the Tallgrass Prairie: An Illustrated Manual for Iowa and the Upper Midwest* (Iowa City, Iowa: University of Iowa Press, 1994), 126, 127.

p. 93. May Sarton, *Recovering: A Journal 1978-1979* (New York: W.W. Norton & Company, 1997), 100, quoting from a book *The Journals and Letters of the Little Locksmith.*

p. 96. Garret Keizer, *The Enigma of Anger: Essays on a Sometimes Deadly Sin* (San Francisco, Jossey Bass, A Wiley Company, 2002), 42.

p. 97. Ephesians 6, *The Message,* Eugene Peterson (Colorado Springs, Colorado: NavPress, 1993, 1994, 1995).

p. 99. Brennan Manning, *The Wisdom of Tenderness: What Happens When God's Fierce Mercy Transforms Our Lives* (New York: HarperCollins, HarperSanFrancisco, 2002), 122.

p. 99. Kathleen Norris, *The Cloister Walk* (New York: G.P. Putnam & Sons, Riverhead, 1996), 165, 166.

p. 100. Eugene Peterson, *Where Your Treasure Is: Psalms that Summon You from Self to Community* (Grand Rapids, Michigan: Wm. B. Eerdmans, 1993), 14. He is writing here about the correlation between the personal and the public.

p. 100. PhyllisTickle, *The Divine Hours* (New York: Doubleday, 2000, 2001), Compline.

p. 100. Garret Keizer, *The Enigma of Anger: Essays on a Sometimes Deadly Sin* (San Francisco: Jossey Bass, A Wiley Company, 2002), 352.

p. 101. Romans 5, from *The Message,* Eugene Peterson (Colorado Springs, Colorado: NavPress, 1995), 214.

p. 101. Psalm 79:8, *New Jerusalem Bible* (New York: Doubleday, 1985).

p. 102. *The Book of Common Prayer and Administration of the Sacraments and Other Rites and Ceremonies of the Church (Together with the Psalter or Psalms of David according to the use of The Episcopal Church),* (The Seabury Press), 135.

CHAPTER TEN
Prairie Burn: Pain

p. 104. Annick Smith, *Big Bluestem: Journey into the Tall Grass* (Tulsa, Oklahoma: Council Oak Books, The Nature Conservancy, 1996), 84.

p. 104. Margaret Silf, *Inner Compass: An Invitation to Ignatian Spirituality* (Chicago: Loyola Press, Jesuit Way, 1999), 124.

p. 105. Mary Oliver, "Hummingbird Pauses at the Trumpet Vine," *New and Selected Poems* (Boston: Beacon Press, 1992), 56.

p. 107. Psalm 90:5,6, from the Psalter, *The Book of Common Prayer and Administration of the Sacraments and Other Rites and Ceremonies of the Church (Together with the Psalter or Psalms of David according to the use of The Episcopal Church),* (The Seabury Press), 718.

p. 108. 1 Corinthians 15:55, *Holy Bible: New Living Translation* (Wheaton, Illinois: Tyndale House Publishers, 1996).

p. 108. 1 Corinthians 7:31, *The Message,* Eugene Peterson (Colorado Springs, Colorado: NavPress, 1995).

p. 109. Richard Manning, *Grassland: The History, Biology, Politics, and Promise of the American Prairie* (New York: Penguin, 1995), 282.

p. 109. Psalm 103:15,16, *Holy Bible: New Living Translation* (Wheaton, Illinois: Tyndale House Publishers, 1996).

p. 110. This memorable phrase was the despairing cry of the Wicked Witch of the West after Dorothy threw water on her and she melted into oblivion, in the classic movie *The Wizard of Oz* (Warner Studios, 1939), based on the Oz series by L. Frank Baum.

p. 110. Jane Kenyon, *A Hundred White Daffodils* (Saint Paul, Minnesota: Graywolf Press, 1999), 85.

p. 112. C.S. Lewis, *The Weight of Glory* (New York: Simon & Schuster, 1996), 31.

p. 112. Psalm 90:12, *King James Version.*

p. 113. May Sarton, *Recovering: A Journal 1978-1979* (New York: W.W. Norton & Company, 1997), 209.

p. 116. Lorraine Kisly, ed., *Watch and Pray* (New York: Random House, Inc., Crown Publishing Group,), 220, quoting Hugh of Balma.

CHAPTER ELEVEN
Sandhill Cranes: Joy

p. 118. This ancient Chinese proverb was one I ran across in Diane Ackerman's beautiful book *A Natural History of the Senses* (New York: Random House Inc., Vintage Books, 1990), 193.

p. 118. Phyllis Tickle, *The Divine Hours, Prayers for Summertime* (New York: Doubleday, 2000), xv, quoting St. Augustine.

p. 122. Michael Card, *Scribbling in the Sand: Christ and Creativity* (Downers Grove, Illinois: InterVarsity Press, 2002), 51.

p. 122. Psalm 13:5,6, *The Message,* Eugene Peterson (Colorado Springs, Colorado: NavPress, 1995).

p. 124. Peter Matthiessen, *Birds of Heaven* (New York: Ferrar, Straus and Giroux, North Point Press, 2001), 3, 4.

CHAPTER TWELVE
Twilight: Creativity

p. 126. John Madson, *Where the Sky Began: Land of the Tallgrass Prairie* (Ames, Iowa: Iowa State University Press, 1982, 1995), quoting Emily Dickinson.

p. 126. Evelyn Underhill, *Practical Mysticism* (Great Britain: Eagle, 1991), 96.

p. 130. Greg Breining, *Wild Shore: Exploring Lake Superior by Kayak* (Minneapolis, Minnesota: University of Minnesota Press, 2000), 21, quoting anthropologist Thor Conway in *Painted Dreams.*

p. 131. James Russell Lowell, as quoted on the Web site [www.conservativeforum.org]. It doesn't seem to be from a book; most likely it is from a speech.

p. 131. Evelyn Underhill, *Practical Mysticism* (Great Britian: Eagle, 1991), 96.

CHAPTER THIRTEEN
Conservationists: Mentors

p. 134. Walt Whitman, "Song of Myself," *Leaves of Grass* (New York: Bantam Doubleday Dell, 1983), 47.

p. 134. Lorraine Kisly, ed., *Watch and Pray: Christian Teachings on the Practice of Prayer* (New York: Random House, Inc., Crown Publishing Group, Bell Tower, 2002), 227, quoting Teresa of Avila.

CHAPTER FOURTEEN
After the Rain: Mystery

p. 140. Diane Ackerman, *A Natural History of the Senses* (New York: Random House, Inc., Vintage Books, 1990), 309.

p. 140. Belden C. Lane, *The Solace of Fierce Landscapes: Exploring Desert and Mountain Spirituality* (New York: Oxford University Press, 1998), 65.

p. 142. Henry Mitchell, *The Essential Earthman* (Bloomington, Indiana: Indiana University Press, 1981), 18.

p. 143. Evelyn Underhill, *Practical Mysticism* (Great Britain: Eagle, 1991), 85.

p. 146. David James Duncan, *My Story as Told by Water: Confessions, Druidic Rants, Reflections, Bird-Watchings, Fish-Stalkings, Visions, Songs and Prayers Refracting Light, from Living Rivers, in the Age of the Industrial Dark* (Berkeley, California: University of California Press, 2001), 81, quoting Henry Bugbee.

EPIGRAPH

Annick Smith, *Big Bluestem: Journey into the Tallgrass* (Tulsa, Oklahoma: Council Oak Books, The Nature Conservancy, 1996), 282.

ACKNOWLEDGMENTS

None of my writing would happen without the support of my husband and dearest friend, Jeff, who loves, encourages, comforts, and advises. My two teenagers, Dustin and Jennifer, are patient with my writing jags and good at giving hugs when I'm discouraged. I love you.

My editor and dear friend Lil Copan saw promise in my early rough scribblings and helped me shape them into what you see here. I cannot overestimate what she has contributed through her advice, mentoring, and editing skills. Thank you, Lil.

Lillian Miao and the good folks of the Community of Jesus and at Paraclete Press have extended their hospitality to me in ways too numerous to mention. It's a privilege to learn from them both in my writing and in my spiritual life. Thanks for providing me with a time of rest and refreshment in the beautiful landscape of Cape Cod.

My parents, Bill and Carolyn Strafford, gave me every opportunity as a child to read and develop my creative bent. Mom and Dad, you're the best! Thanks also to my "other mom," Nancy Crosby.

This book would not have been possible without a large community of friends who have graciously served as sounding boards: my writing pals Lisa McMinn and Camerin Courtney; book buddies Alice Fryling,

Ruth Bamford, Zondra Lindblade, and Ewan Russell; and my dear friends and fellow writers LaVonne Neff and Vinita Hampton Wright. I'm exceedingly grateful to Dwight Baker, who first told me about the prairie landscape and loaned me many of the books I've referenced here. The writings of Phyllis Tickle and Robert Benson nurtured me each day as I learned the habits of fixed-hour prayer; I count them both as friends and am eternally in their debt for their words. Thanks also to Paul Gruchow, whose writing has taught me so much about faith and the outdoors.

The Schulenberg Prairie is truly one of the jewels of the Chicago region. It would not be with us if not for Ray Schulenberg's untiring and visionary efforts to bring back the tallgrass prairie, and also the commitment and funding of the Morton Arboretum. The prairie owes much to the work of countless volunteers, supervised by Craig Johnson, the prairie manager and Director of External Affairs. It's a privilege to learn from these folks, and I will be forever grateful for the place of solace the prairie has been to me.

Thanks also to Craig Johnson, who read this manuscript for accuracy concerning the Schulenberg Prairie. His gracious input saved me from many an embarrassing gaffe; any remaining errors are my own.

Like a sponge, I soaked up many writings that I mention in the endnotes and am endlessly indebted to the authors for their insights. If I have inadvertently replicated their thoughts here without crediting them, it was not by intention, just by osmosis. They have helped me grow, and I am grateful.

The staff of the Morton Arboretum bookstore and gift shop have been a constant encouragement to me as I wrote this book. The folks who run The Book Store in downtown Glen Ellyn offered their support as well, as did the Borders bookstore in Wheaton and Family Bookstore in Plainfield, Indiana. Craig Stoll of Mardel gave my first book a boost when it needed one, as did Rebecca Gorczyca and my dear friends at all of the Logos Bookstores. Amazon's former religion editor Katherine Koberg and former spirituality editor Gail Hudson were also a terrific encouragement. Bless you all.

And as always, my utmost thanks to the staff at Caribou Coffee in Glen Ellyn, Illinois, who refilled my coffee mug with endless cappuccinos and let me take up table space over the course of a year as I wrote this book: Daniel, Emily, Barb, Sarah Kueker, Sara Scott, Erika, Gemma, Mallory, Megan McCluskey, Megan McMinn, Liz, Erin Markley, Erin Emerson, Ryan, Natalie, Anne, Nate, Jessica, and Jeff. They also gave me hints if I didn't know the answer to the daily trivia question, and often snuck a little bit of chocolate into my cappuccinos. I appreciate you.

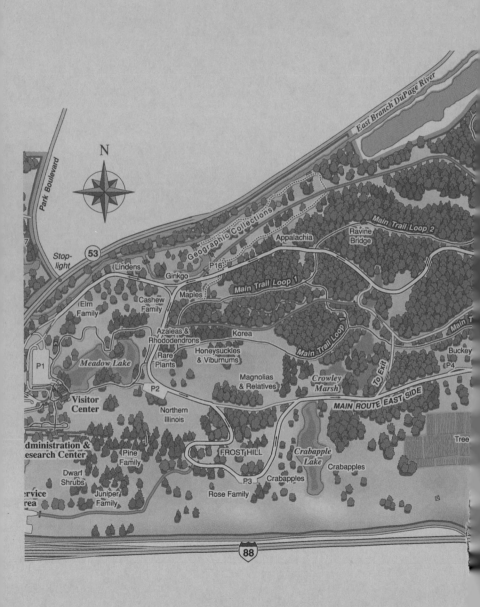